VISUAL
LITERACY
FOR LIBRARIES

ALA Editions purchases fund advocacy, awareness, and accreditation programs for library professionals worldwide.

VISUAL LITERACY
FOR LIBRARIES

A PRACTICAL, STANDARDS-BASED GUIDE

Nicole E. Brown

Kaila Bussert

Denise Hattwig

Ann Medaille

An imprint of the American Library Association

CHICAGO 2016

© 2016 by Nicole E. Brown, Kaila Bussert, Denise Hattwig, and Ann Medaille

Extensive effort has gone into ensuring the reliability of the information in this book; however, the publisher makes no warranty, express or implied, with respect to the material contained herein.

ISBN: 978-0-8389-1381-9 (paper)

Library of Congress Cataloging-in-Publication Data

Names: Brown, Nicole E., author. | Bussert, Kaila, author. | Hattwig, Denise, author. | Medaille, Ann, author.
Title: Visual literacy for libraries : a practical, standards-based guide / Nicole E. Brown, Kaila Bussert, Denise Hattwig, Ann Medaille.
Description: Chicago : ALA Editions, an imprint of the American Library Association, 2016. | Includes bibliographical references and index.
Identifiers: LCCN 2015033082 | ISBN 9780838913819 (print : alk. paper)
Subjects: LCSH: Information literacy—Study and teaching (Higher)—Activity programs. | Visual literacy—Study and teaching (Higher)—Activity programs. | Pictures—Research. | Visual communication. | Academic libraries—Relations with faculty and curriculum.
Classification: LCC ZA3075 .B77 2016 | DDC 028.7071/1—dc23 LC record available at http://lccn.loc.gov/2015033082

Cover design by Alejandra Diaz. Book design by Kim Thornton in the Tisa Pro and Interstate typefaces.

♾ This paper meets the requirements of ANSI/NISO Z39.48–1992 (Permanence of Paper).

Printed in the United States of America
20 19 18 17 16   5 4 3 2 1

CONTENTS

Preface ix

Acknowledgments xi

Introduction xiii

3   Create and Use Images   65

4   Ethical Use of Images   103

PREFACE

IN FEBRUARY 2013 during a meeting of the Association of College and Research Libraries (ACRL) Visual Literacy Task Force, which we comprise, an agenda item read, "Next VLTF project." We wanted to help academic librarians learn to apply, teach, and promote visual literacy, and we brainstormed ways to do this. By the fall of 2014 we were writing *Visual Literacy for Libraries*.

This book came out of a truly collaborative process: we wrote it *together*. This is not an edited volume or an anthology—this is a coauthored work, jointly conceived and collectively written. Each of us brings a unique perspective to visual literacy, and we felt that this was the best way to reflect our range of experiences and create a cohesive whole. Instead of divvying up chapters or sections, we worked to develop a unified voice. We adopted such practices as using a common language for each phase of writing; we like the Madman (we call it Mad*woman*, of course)–Architect–Carpenter–Judge model introduced by Betty S. Flowers in a 1981 *Language Arts* piece on roles in the writing process. We wrote in assigned colors (Nicole, pink; Denise, blue; Kaila, purple; Ann, maroon) to signal when we were in true "hashing it out mode," making our thought processes as apparent as we could to each other. As we coedited the prose, we collaboratively decided when to turn the text to black, meaning we all signed off (at least for the stage we were in). As we wrote, we generated an authorial voice that is uniquely "ours," different than any one of us would have done alone, and certainly richer.

ACKNOWLEDGMENTS

WE'D LIKE TO thank our families, friends, colleagues, and each other.

We are also grateful to Russ White, data and GIS specialist at California Polytechnic State University San Luis Obispo's Robert E. Kennedy Library, for his insights and contributions to the ideas, visuals, and activities about data interpretation and data visualization. His expertise and experience working with students at a polytechnic university helped us grapple with the nuances of interpreting and evaluating data, and strengthened our thinking about using a critical visual and information literacy lens to examine data visualizations. He is a passionate advocate for helping students access, explore, and share all types of data in their academic work, and we genuinely appreciate his collaborative collegiality.

INTRODUCTION

VISUAL LITERACY HAS a long history and means different things to different people. As we've worked with visual literacy over the past decade (some of us more, some less), we've heard lots of different takes on what visual literacy is all about. We've heard that it is only for art historians or graphic designers and that librarians shouldn't be involved. We've seen presentations that equate visual literacy with art appreciation. We've encountered befuddled looks from librarians wondering what we're talking about . . . and why?

Why Visual Literacy and Academic Libraries?

When we step back and think about how to situate visual literacy into a library context, the word *critical* keeps coming up: critical thinking, critical viewing, critical using, critical making, and the list goes on. To understand our approach, start with your own practice, add images, and see where it takes you.

> Do you encourage students to think critically as they research?
>> How can you extend this experience to images?
> Do you embrace critical information literacy?
>> Can you bring visual content to enrich that experience?
> Do you teach students to critically evaluate sources?
>> How can you expand that practice to images?

You'll see a lot of questions in this book, because our approach is inquiry-driven. This is not to say that we don't cover the basics of image content. Curious about color? Covered. Not sure where to find great images? We'll show you. Wondering what makes a good presentation? We talk about that too. But what we really want you to get out of this book is a new understanding of how images fit into our critical (there it is again) practice as librarians and how we can advance student learning with our own visual literacy.

This book grounds visual literacy in your everyday practice—connecting it to what you know and do as a librarian who engages in reflective practice. Heidi Jacobs put it well when she argued that, for information literacy pedagogy, "one of the best ways for us to encourage students to be engaged learners is for us to become engaged learners, delve deeply into our own problem posing, and embody the kind of engagement we want to see in our students" (Jacobs 2008). We extend this viewpoint to visual literacy pedagogy and provide many opportunities for you to embody the kind of visual literacy that you want to develop in your learners.

What Is Visual Literacy?

At this point, you probably want a definition for visual literacy. The following definition is set forth in the ACRL *Visual Literacy Competency Standards for Higher Education* (see the appendix for the complete standards):

> Visual literacy is a set of abilities that enables an individual to effectively find, interpret, evaluate, use, and create images and visual media. Visual literacy enables a learner to understand and analyze the contextual, cultural, ethical, aesthetic, intellectual, and technical components involved in the production and use of visual materials. A visually literate individual is both a critical consumer of visual media and a competent contributor to a body of shared knowledge and culture. (ACRL 2011)

The **Visual Literacy array** expresses this definition graphically.

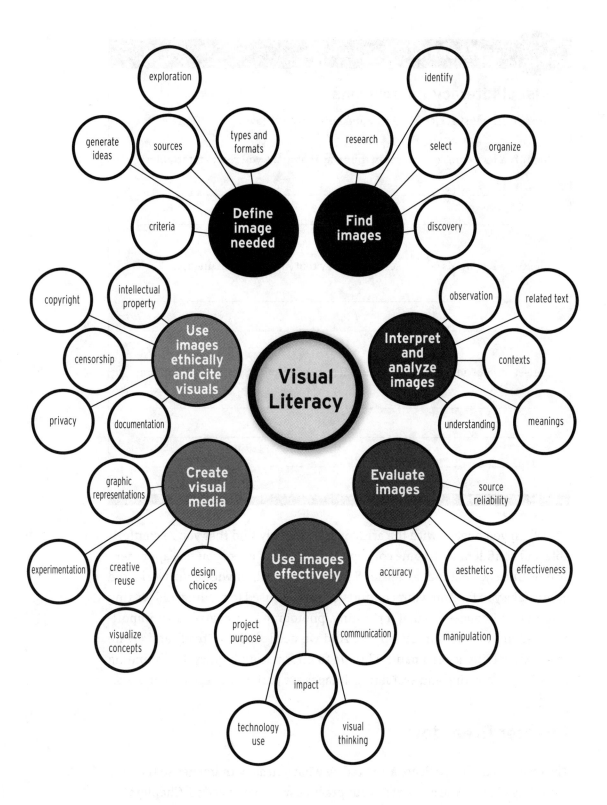

Based on ACRL's Visual Literacy Standards by D. Hattwig, K. Bussert, and A. Medaille. Copyright 2013, Johns Hopkins University Press. This image first appeared in *portal: Libraries and the Academy*, Volume 13, Issue 1, January 2013, p. 75.

COFFEE BREAK!

Visual Literacy Impressions

Examine the Visual Literacy Array and answer the following questions:

Identify a few words or phrases in the array that make you feel comfortable:

_____

_____

Identify a few words or phrases in the array that make you feel uneasy:

_____

_____

Reflect on your answers. Which visual literacy concepts do you want to explore?

_____

_____

_____

When you engage with the array, you'll probably find that you're comfortable and confident with some concepts, while others make you feel apprehensive or uneasy. That makes sense! Some concepts align with your work, and others take you far from your comfort zone. We're used to reading and writing text, but an image—whether a painting, photograph, or chart—is an important medium of communication too. And we need skills to "read" and create them. Visual literacy is a natural bridge to information literacy. From finding and using to creating and evaluating, images are part of the research process.

Chapter Breakdown

The chapters in this book are arranged by what you *do* with images so that you can easily connect the content to your practice when you need to. Chapters 1–5 focus on components of visual literacy, while chapter 6 steps back and looks at visual literacy from a wider angle.

Chapter 1: Interpret and Analyze Images builds fluency with unpacking the meanings of images and visual media.

Chapter 2: Find the Right Images points to sources and practices for finding great images.

Chapter 3: Create and Use Images builds a repertoire of skills for crafting visual communication.

Chapter 4: Ethical Use of Images considers the ethical implications of creating, sharing, and using image content.

Chapter 5: Cite and Credit Images provides tips and templates for giving credit to image creators in scholarly and creative work.

Chapter 6: Images and the Research Process connects images to the larger process of information literacy and the *ACRL Framework for Information Literacy for Higher Education.*

How to Use This Book

This book is meant to be *used,* and you don't have to read it cover to cover. Here are some tips to make the most out of this book's features and empower you to skip around with purpose.

Foundational Questions: Every chapter begins with a set of foundational questions that can be used as prompts for the full process of working with visual materials. Use these questions in the classroom, or parse them out in discussions with students, colleagues, and faculty.

Coffee Breaks: We've heard from many of you that you want to develop your own visual literacy, but you don't know where to begin. Our Coffee Breaks are designed just for you! These short, self-contained, low-stakes activities can be completed at your desk. They are also fun to do with a partner, with a learning community, or in a professional development session. Jump to any Coffee Break for a chance to pause, reflect, and apply visual literacy to your practice.

More to Explore: Look for these lists of resources to learn more about the topics covered in each chapter and to stay up-to-date with new developments. These lists can be great starting points for developing your own visual literacy resources guides.

Visual Literacy in Action: Each chapter ends with a Visual Literacy in Action section filled with practical, outcomes-driven activities for you to use in your everyday work with students. Use the activities as is, or adapt them to suit your context. Reflect on the activities by capturing your observations about student learning: What evidence of learning was there? Where did students get stuck? How might you revise the activities?

Most of all, have fun! Use our ready-to-go activities, strategies, and ideas to begin working with images. As you support students' acquisition of visual literacy, you'll also learn how to use visual materials to make your instruction more engaging. Or, maybe you'll create a presentation that wows an audience. Whatever your visual literacy goal, this book will give you specific tools to knock it out of the park when you discuss, teach, and practice visual literacy.

REFERENCES

ACRL (Association of College and Research Libraries). 2011. *ACRL Visual Literacy Competency Standards for Higher Education*. www.ala.org/acrl/standards/visualliteracy.

Jacobs, Heidi. 2008. "Information Literacy and Reflective Pedagogical Praxis." *Journal of Academic Librarianship* 34 (3): 256–62.

Interpret and Analyze Images

EWS STORIES OCCASIONALLY remind us that image interpretation and analysis skills are essential. In 2010, the United States Postal Service (USPS) issued a Statue of Liberty Forever Stamp featuring an image of a replica of the Statue of Liberty from the New York-New York Hotel and Casino in Las Vegas—not the Statue of Liberty in New York Harbor. A stamp dealer discovered the mistake, and the collectors' magazine *Linn's Stamp News* reported that the photograph, selected from Getty Images by the USPS, was accompanied by metadata clearly identifying it as the Las Vegas replica. How could this happen with such an iconic monument? Chances are that applying some of the approaches in this chapter could have headed off the mistake. Strategies such as looking carefully, reading the metadata and textual information associated with the image, and discussing with others could have prevented the mistake. Images are all around us, and we're accustomed to casually glancing at pictures and assuming we know what they are and what they mean. The USPS incident is a good reminder to take the time to *look, read, examine, describe,* and *check understanding.*

This chapter sets forth a flexible process for interpreting and analyzing visual content that you can apply in your work with students as they begin to analyze the meanings of images and visual media. Use our adaptable, inquiry-based process in consultations, instruction sessions, and assignment design.

Through systematic looking, thinking, and questioning, students can come to a solid understanding of the way meaning is produced in images. Some activities in this chapter provide entry points for interpreting and analyzing images, and others move into the deeper consideration of images needed for advanced academic work. Activities range from analyzing photographs to reflecting on the implications of image manipulation. The images, activities, and examples in this chapter can be adapted to align with different disciplinary contexts and levels and to inform partnerships with faculty as you embed visual literacy concepts into the curriculum.

Foundational Questions

How Do I Begin Interpreting and Analyzing?

Start by looking closely at images and asking yourself a few key questions. We offer a flexible, five-step process for interpreting and analyzing visual content. The process begins with learning to look at an image and moves through incorporating textual information, thinking more deeply about meaning, and reflecting on how to further your understanding.

What about Cultural and Social Context?

All images carry meanings that can only be understood through a contextualization of how, when, where, and why they were produced. Images do not exist in a vacuum. Situate images within the framework of their social, political, and economic circumstances.

How Do I Interpret Graphical Information?

To dig deeper into data visualizations, begin by observing and describing the way the data are being presented. Then, ask questions about the data: Who produced the data? Are the data reliable? What methods were used? Consider the audience, purpose, and effectiveness of visual design as you interpret graphical information.

What Does the Text That Accompanies Images Tell Me?

When interpreting and analyzing images, the text you read alongside the images furthers your analysis by telling you more about those images. Use text to gain valuable context about *where, how, why,* and *for whom* the image was created. Text may also reveal that an image is part of a larger collection or let you know who holds the image rights.

What Do I Need to Know about Image Alterations and Manipulation?

Has the image you're looking at been edited and altered? Changes to image files can have significant implications for their meaning, authenticity, and reliability. A general awareness of common image manipulations will help you know what to look out for.

Getting Started: Looking and Interpreting

Careful looking is the essential first step in image interpretation. We encounter so many images in our daily lives that a quick glance is usually all we have time for. When using images in academic work, however, a quick glance does not give us the information we need and can lead to misinterpretation and misuse. Developing the patience to look closely at an image can take practice, and **Activity 1.1: Learning to Look** gives you the opportunity to walk through this process.

The beginning of a typical library instruction session is an excellent time to present an engaging opening activity using images. Images related to

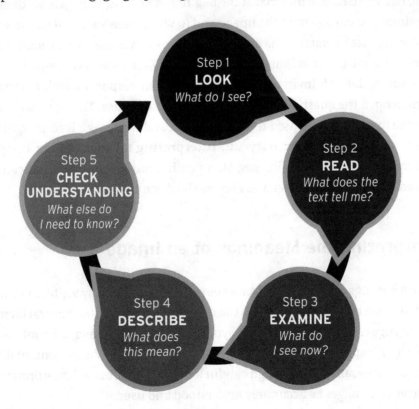

Figure 1.1. *Interpreting and Analyzing Images*

COFFEE BREAK!

Begin to Interpret and Analyze an Image

Choose an image and take a few minutes to look at it closely. Answer the questions, then reflect.

What do I see?

What is going on?

Why do I think this image was created?

REFLECT

What do you want to know more about?

How might you put this exercise into practice?

course content coupled with a few "looking prompts" can get students in a question-driven mind-set and frame the research process. Try projecting an image related to course material at the beginning of class, then give students a few minutes to engage with the image and to write answers to questions such as: *What do I see? What is going on? Why do I think this image was created?* After students spend a few minutes freewriting answers, use a think-pair-share technique to debrief. Invite students to share their responses with a partner and then open the questions for the whole class to discuss. This approach sets the stage for an inquiry-based research session and works as a lead-in to more pointed visual analysis. **Activity 1.2: Interpreting and Analyzing Images** provides a comprehensive process, along with question prompts that can be adapted for instructional scenarios across the disciplines.

Interpreting the Meanings of an Image

Image meanings are shaped by factors beyond what is initially visible. The historical and social contexts in which the image was created, and cultural factors such as suggestion, metaphor, and symbols within the image, all contribute to the significance and communicative value of an image. Visual content does not stand alone, and only through careful looking and informed interpretation practices can images be accurately understood and used.

CULTURAL AND SOCIAL CONTEXT

To understand the richness of images as information sources, students need to situate images in their cultural, social, and historical contexts. You can sharpen students' image interpretation skills by regularly using examples of images that differ in terms of time period, medium, and subject matter and by guiding students through the process of looking carefully and making sense of what they see. By learning to interpret images in various contexts, students gain a deeper understanding of visual content and prepare to think about incorporating images into research papers and projects.

Understanding the context of an image includes thinking critically about how the image represents people—both as individuals and as representatives or signifiers of different groups. Image interpretation skills help students to arrive at an informed, nuanced, and historically contextualized understanding of diversity and difference across cultural groups and identifications and among individuals within those groups. Images are also excellent sources for research projects that focus on historical or diversity-related issues because they often contain gender, ethnic, and other cultural or social identifiers, cues, or stereotypes. Visual literacy interpretation practices equip students to approach looking with a critical eye when they encounter images of people different from themselves, and advance students' research process through accurate and informed analysis of representations.

Use classroom activities to generate discussions about how individuals and groups are depicted in images. Discussions can focus on the relationships among people and objects within the image, the social and economic status of individuals or groups represented, and the use of suggestion and symbolism to portray cultural identifiers. An excellent source for images to generate such discussion is the blog *Sociological Images* by Lisa Wade, a sociology professor at Occidental College. With over five thousand posts consisting of an image alongside content analysis, Wade's blog aims to encourage people "to exercise and develop their sociological imagination by presenting brief . . . discussions of compelling and timely imagery that span the breadth of sociological inquiry" (Wade n.d.).

Advertisements are another rich source of content for deepening image analysis skills. Exploring the images, layout, and other design choices in ads sharpens visual literacy skills while helping students to think about historical context. You might lead students to ads related to specific time periods, products, or services and then launch into a targeted discussion. Subscription databases, such as ProQuest Historical Newspapers, and free resources, such as Duke University Library's Ad*Access project, are excellent sources for

Key Questions for Ad Analysis

- Where does your eye go? Why?
- What is the relationship between the text and the image?
- What ambience or mood does this ad create?
- What might it have been like to see this ad when it came out?
- What does this ad tell you about the ideal (look, role, relationship, etc.) of the time?
- What role do you think this product played in the culture and society in which it was created?
- What sociological, political, economic, or cultural attitudes are reflected in this ad?

historical advertisements. When used in the classroom with our **Key Questions for Ad Analysis,** historical ads build analysis skills while setting the stage for further research. **Activity 1.3: Analyzing an Ad for Context** situates ad analysis in a library context and uses visual literacy as a bridge to information literacy.

SUGGESTION AND METAPHOR

Images are representations that contain meanings beyond the literal, and an image's impact can come from the use of suggestion or metaphor. For example, an image of a lion evokes the literal or primary meaning of a large, orange-colored member of the cat family. However, the same image of a lion might evoke a feeling such as fear or awe, or suggest an idea such as power, importance, or strength. The suggestive or metaphorical meaning derived from images is influenced by the context in which the image is presented and by the type of image used. Thus, an image of a lion that is situated next to an image of a mouse may suggest one meaning while the same image that is situated next to text that reads "It's a jungle out there!" will suggest another. Similarly, an image of a roaring lion will suggest a meaning that is different from that of a sitting lion, a yawning lion, or a napping lion.

Sometimes images are repeatedly associated with an idea or concept and may come to take on symbolic meaning. So if you've ever seen an image of a lion and thought "king," or seen an image of a dove and thought "peace," it may be because these animals have been traditionally associated with the idea of a king or peace, not because a lion is a sovereign over other animals or because a dove seeks to create harmony. The interpretation of visual signs, symbols, and their meanings may vary depending on one's cultural background or life experience,

MORE TO EXPLORE: IMAGE INTERPRETATION AND ANALYSIS

NARA Document Analysis Worksheets

www.archives.gov/education/lessons/worksheets

The National Archives and Records Administration's education staff provides structured worksheets for analyzing photographs, cartoons, posters, and maps.

LOC Teacher's Guides and Analysis Tool

www.loc.gov/teachers/usingprimarysources/guides.html

The Library of Congress provides analysis tools for primary sources, photographs, manuscripts, sheet music, and more.

NASA: How to Interpret a Satellite Image

http://earthobservatory.nasa.gov/Features/ColorImage

NASA Earth Observatory's writers and data visualizers provide tips and strategies for understanding satellite images.

or the context in which the image is used. For instance, the peace sign might symbolize antiwar sentiments for some or an alternative to waving goodbye for others. Taking a critical approach to investigating the construction of meaning in images is an essential component of image interpretation and analysis.

Visualizing Data

Visual representations of data and information let us see relationships, patterns, and trends we may not easily see otherwise. Data visualizations are central to scientific inquiry and communication because they aid in understanding complex information quickly and efficiently. Statistician Francis Anscombe demonstrated the extent to which visualizations can provide critical insight into the qualities of data with his four data sets known as Anscombe's quartet (Anscombe 1973). Although his data sets have nearly identical statistical properties, they appear very different when presented as graphs because the data contain variations. Visualizations, in other words, reveal important aspects of the data that might otherwise be overlooked. Visualizations can also elicit new insights—for example, when statistical information (quantitative data) is displayed on a map or when the number of words from a textual corpus (qualitative data) is processed as a word cloud.

COFFEE BREAK!

Interpret a Visual Sign or Symbol

Walk around your library (or look at the website) and select a sign or symbol that you encounter. Then answer the following questions.

What sign or symbol did you choose?

What does it represent to you?

Why?

What might the sign or symbol represent to a person who:

   Is a new student?

   Has never been to your library?

   Saw it two hundred years ago?

   Sees it two hundred years from now?

REFLECT

What did you learn from this process?

How might you apply this process to your work?

Though visualizations make quantitative information easier to understand, interpreting and analyzing them requires some instruction and practice. In a review of graph comprehension research, psychologists Shah and Hoeffner (2002) contend that three important factors impact how well someone interprets graphic information: (1) the visual characteristics of the graph, (2) general knowledge about graphs and how they function, and (3) the person's prior knowledge and beliefs about the content. Shah and Hoeffner argue that to improve graph comprehension educators should train students to apply metacognition and "think of graph reading as an interpretation and evaluation task as opposed to a mere fact retrieval task" (2002, 64). **Activity 1.5: Evaluating Data Visualizations in the News** takes students through this interpretation and evaluation process by engaging with a real-world news example in which graphs are used to explain a societal trend.

Because being a successful reader of data visualizations depends upon knowing what to look for and what questions to ask, we provide **Twenty Key Questions for Interpreting and Evaluating Data Visualizations.** The questions are divided into three stages: observation and description, interpretation, and evaluation. For example, two of our key questions ask students to articulate general knowledge about graphs so that they can practice identifying the format and situating it within a schema that categorizes data visualizations according to the communication goal. This exercise positions students to recognize the type of graph with a description of its basic purpose (e.g., *This is a bar chart, which is useful for comparing values across categories*). Students will begin to grasp that one type of visualization is not necessarily better than another; rather, each has its strengths and limitations. The following sections show common communication purposes alongside a typical example for visualizing data based on the purpose.

COMPARE VALUES ACROSS CATEGORIES

Example: Bar Chart

A bar chart uses rectangular bars, plotted vertically or horizontally, with the height or length showing each value.

Strengths

- Provides a quick comparison of values across categories
- Conveys the maximum, minimum, and relative ranking of the categories being compared

Limitations

- Can provide an incomplete or simplified view of the data
- May imply, but not actually reveal, trends and patterns

Other Examples: Horizontal Bar Chart, Stacked Bar Chart

SHOW PARTS OF A WHOLE

Example: Pie Chart

A pie chart is a circle divided into sections that represent proportions of the whole.

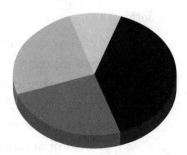

Strengths

- Shows a percentage or proportion, also known as a *part-to-the-whole* relationship
- Familiar format to a wide audience

Limitations

- Less effective when there is a large number of categories
- Difficult to discern small differences between categories
- Difficult to illustrate trends over time using a series of pie charts

Other Examples: Stacked Bar Chart

SHOW CHANGES OVER TIME

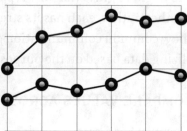

Example: Line Chart
A line chart or line graph uses a line
to connect a series of data points.

Strengths

- Shows change over time, or historical trends, when plotted in a time series
- Can compare different data series or multiple lines in the same time
  frame

Limitations

- More difficult to interpret when comparing multiple lines or series
- Aspect ratio (height and width) can influence the appearance of the
  lines and interpretation of the chart

Other Examples: Area Chart, Stacked Area Chart

SHOW RELATIONSHIP BETWEEN VARIABLES

Example: Scatter Plot
A scatter plot (also spelled scatterplot) is a
set of data points plotted on the x and y axes.

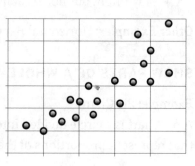

Strengths

- Used to explore relationships or
  trends between two variables
- Can illustrate many different aspects
  of the plotted data, such as:
  - ◊ Correlation between variables (and whether the correlation is
    positive or negative)
  - ◊ Variation of the data (clear trend or scattered)
  - ◊ Nature of the relationship (linear or nonlinear)
  - ◊ Identification of outliers
- In statistics, used for evaluating a line of best fit

Limitations
- Displays only two variables at a time (may not provide a full picture for data sets with many variables)

Other Examples: 3D Scatter Plot, Bubble Chart

TELL A STORY ABOUT A COMPLEX ISSUE

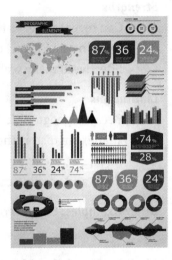

Example: Infographics
Infographics present information and data, often combining multiple forms of visualizations, to illustrate a topic in a concise, engaging, and aesthetically pleasing manner.

Strengths
- Can show a variety of data in relatively small and succinct visual forms
- Uses data to present a narrative or advocate for a position

Limitations
- Can be "busy" and difficult to read
- Presents data selectively and therefore can be biased
- Emphasizes the story over a comprehensive view of the data
- Design choices and templates can compromise accuracy

SHOW CONNECTIONS

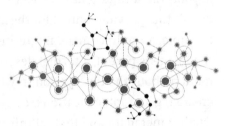

Example: Network Diagram
A network diagram consists of a set of nodes and connecting lines.

Strengths
- Illustrates the connections or links between people or things
- Size, shape, and position of lines and nodes indicate the type and strength of relationships

Limitations
- Often requires interactivity to present large and complex data sets
- Can require specialized knowledge of network analysis for understanding

Other Examples: Arc Diagram, Flow Chart, Organizational Chart

SHOW GEOGRAPHIC DISTRIBUTION

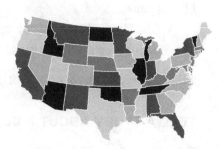

Example: Choropleth Map
A choropleth map uses colors and shading to represent quantities within defined geographic areas.

Strengths

- Can reveal patterns that may not be clear in other forms of visualization
- Effective at many scales, from local to global, with suitable geographic data

Limitations

- Because geographic boundaries are not typically uniform in size and shape, can distort the visual significance of areas represented on the map (e.g., the size of Texas versus Rhode Island)
- Color and shading can affect interpretation of the map

Other Examples: Contour or Isopleth Maps, Dot Maps, Heat Maps

Using Text to Understand Images

Taking the time to read captions, metadata, and other text that accompanies an image gives you essential information you cannot get from simply looking at the image. Just as reading a catalog record for a book reveals information beyond the author and title, examining the text alongside an image fills in details that provide context for the image and further the research process. For example, an online image might include information about a collection that the image is part of, a formal description, names of the rights holders, information about the time period in which the image (or its representation) was created, geographic locations, or even the process used to create the image. Quality metadata and textual information provide essential context such as *why, where, how,* and *for whom* the image was created.

The level of description tells you a lot about an image and its source, and what's *not* there can also tell you something about the image or raise additional questions. Somebody—whether the image creator herself, using natural language, or a visual resource cataloger at a cultural heritage institution, using a fixed taxonomy—took the time to generate the descriptions you find. Tags and metadata can indicate aspects of the image that were important to the image creator, image provider, or commentator. As a researcher, noticing these textual clues (or lack thereof) is crucial for critically engaging with visual

Twenty Key Questions for Interpreting and Evaluating Data Visualizations

Carefully read the title, description, headings, units, and each part of the key before answering the following questions.

OBSERVE AND DESCRIBE

What information is being presented?

1. What components or variables are presented?
2. What do the lines, colors, symbols, and so forth represent?
3. What are the units of measure?
4. What trends and patterns do you see?
5. What type of graph or visualization is being used?
6. What are the sources of data?
7. How were the data collected?
8. Were the data modified, analyzed, or summarized?

INTERPRET

What are the meaning and purpose of the data or information presented?

9. What conclusions can you draw from your observations of the data?
10. What is the question, topic, or issue being addressed?
11. What does the data tell you about the issue, and are these findings meaningful?
12. What does the data not tell you, or what are the limitations of the data?

EVALUATE

Are the design and function effective and appropriate?

13. Does the visualization help you understand the data or the broader issue?
14. Do design elements (typography, color, line, etc.) work together to convey the overall message?
15. Is the type of graphic appropriate for the data being presented?
16. Are there better, alternative options to display the data?
17. Are the data and methods reliable and appropriate?
18. Is there a related data set that would add to your understanding of the question, topic, or issue?
19. Are there other visualizations that would add to your understanding of the question, topic, or issue?
20. How might you use this data visualization?

MORE TO EXPLORE: VISUALIZING DATA

Data + Design by Trina Chiasson, Dyanna Gregory, et al., https://infoactive
.co/data-design (CC BY-NC-SA)

Data Points: Visualization That Means Something by Nathan Yau (2013)

Data Visualization: A Successful Design Process by Andy Kirk (2012)

How to Lie with Maps by Mark Monmonier (1996)

Show Me the Numbers: Designing Tables and Graphs to Enlighten by
Stephen Few (2012)

The Visual Display of Quantitative Information by Edward Tufte (2001)

"Visualise Data" in *BetterEvaluation* (blog) by Stephanie Evergreen (2014),
http://betterevaluation.org/plan/describe/visualise_data

*The Wall Street Journal Guide to Information Graphics: The Dos and Don'ts
of Presenting Data, Facts, and Figures* by Dona M. Wong (2010)

content. Questioning the text can also influence what you see in the image and how you see it. Use our **Key Questions for Using Text to Interpret Images** to facilitate discussions about image interpretation and to conduct image analysis. Practice looking closely at image metadata from different sources with **Activity 1.4: Comparing Image Metadata**.

Analyzing Images for Alterations and Editing

Simple image alterations, such as cropping and color correcting, can significantly change an image's meaning. Images have immediate emotional impact and are used in the media and advertising to persuade readers and consumers. This combination of ease-of-editing and direct impact has been exploited in the media with distorted images that convey targeted messages. For example, in a January 31, 2012, news story in *The Guardian*, John Plunkett reported that the UK's Advertising Standards Authority banned a L'Oréal wrinkle cream ad featuring Rachel Weisz, stating that the photograph in the ad "misleadingly exaggerated the performance of the product" because Weisz's skin appeared to be flawless. In France, politicians are addressing a similar concern by proposing required warning labels on photos that have been digitally altered, much like labels on genetically modified food. Israel even has "Photoshop laws," which regulate the use of image alterations in media and advertising. According to an article in *The Atlantic* by Talya Minsberg (May 9, 2012), the Israeli law requires all ads that "use airbrushing, computer editing, or any other form of Photoshop editing to create a slimmer model must clearly state that fact." If you're not an expert at image manipulation, how can you determine whether an image has been digitally altered?

Even if you're looking at a nonadvertising image, or an image that presents itself as factual or documentary, be aware that any image *can* be digitally manipulated. Some research may be required to determine whether it has been. You can be proactive by researching the creator, the production, and the context surrounding the image. Here are some questions you might ask:

- Who created or produced the image?
- Did the image creator or producer have a particular agenda?
- What were the circumstances surrounding the production of the image?
  ◊ Why was it created?
  ◊ How was it distributed?
- Do other depictions of the image subject confirm or conflict with this image?

This thoughtful approach will ensure that you are a critical reader of visual information. **Activity 1.6: Inspecting Scientific Images** concretizes these skills by exploring possible image manipulations, and their consequences, in the production of scientific knowledge.

Key Questions for Using Text to Interpret Images

- How does the textual description relate to your initial observations of the image?
- Based on the text that accompanies it, what do you know about this visual representation?
- What questions remain unanswered about the image's original historical and cultural context (the *who, what, when, where,* and *why*)?
- How might you begin to answer these new questions?
- What keywords, descriptions, or text might help you with further research?
- What sociological, political, economic, or cultural attitudes are reflected in this ad?

Next Steps

Develop interpretation and analysis by looking carefully, reading the textual information associated with images, and discussing what you see with others. To incorporate this strategy into your work in consultation and the classroom, try the following:

- Try our **Five Steps for Interpreting and Analyzing Images** to look at, read, examine, describe, and check understanding for various types of images.
- Use the **Twenty Key Questions for Interpreting and Evaluating Data Visualizations** to observe, describe, interpret, and evaluate graphic presentations of data.

REFERENCES

Anscombe, Francis J. 1973. "Graphs in Statistical Analysis." *American Statistician* 27 (1): 17–21.

Shah, Priti, and James Hoeffner. 2002. "Review of Graph Comprehension Research: Implications for Instruction." *Educational Psychology Review* 14 (1): 47–69.

Wade, Lisa. n.d. *Sociological Images* (blog). http://thesocietypages.org/socimages.

ACTIVITY 1.1

Learning to Look

LEARNING OUTCOMES

- Look carefully at an image and observe content and physical details.
- Describe pictorial, graphic, and aesthetic elements of an image.

DESCRIPTION

Guide students through the practice of dedicated looking, using an image that you provide. Project the image or distribute copies of the image to students. When students have completed looking carefully at the image, they compare observations. Distribute the **Learning to Look Worksheet**, or use the following instructions to lead the activity verbally:

- Look carefully at your image.
- Write down ten details you notice. Include at least one detail from each quadrant of the image. Look for details about people, places, things, color, design, movement, and composition.
- When you have completed your list of details, exchange your list with a classmate and compare your observations. Did you observe the same details?

TIP FOR SUCCESS

- If projecting the image, choose one with high resolution.

OPTIONAL EXTENSION

- Give students different images to work with in step 1, and use step 2 for students to exchange their images *and* observations with a classmate.
    Ask: Can you find every detail your classmate observed? What did you notice that your classmate did not?

VISUAL LITERACY STANDARDS CONNECTION

- ACRL Visual Literacy Standard 3, Performance Indicators 1 and 3

Learning to Look

Step 1: Look carefully at the image.

Record ten details you notice. Include at least one detail from each quadrant of the image. Look for details about people, places, things, color, design, movement, and composition.

II	I
III	IV

Step 2: Exchange your list with a classmate and compare your observations.

Describe a detail that your classmate noticed and that you missed.

_____

_____

_____

_____

Interpreting and Analyzing Images

LEARNING OUTCOMES

- Apply a five-step process to interpret and analyze images.
- Develop questions for further research.

DESCRIPTION

This worksheet provides a flexible and comprehensive approach to interpreting and analyzing images. In an instruction session, students respond to an image by answering as many questions as they can. These questions can be used in consultations with faculty and students, in library instruction sessions, in professional development workshops, and by faculty across the disciplines.

TIP FOR SUCCESS

- If projecting the image, choose one with high resolution.

OPTIONAL EXTENSIONS

- Give students one step at a time. Discuss, then proceed to the next step and repeat.
- Use a jigsaw technique: First form five groups of students. Each group will become "experts" in one step of the process. Then form discussion groups with at least one person from each "expert" group.
- Have students add questions to each step, then discuss.

VISUAL LITERACY STANDARDS CONNECTION

- ACRL Visual Literacy Standard 3, Performance Indicators 1, 2, and 4

Interpreting and Analyzing Images

Here are five steps for interpreting and analyzing images. The approach is iterative and fluid—you may not need to (or be able to) complete each step, or you may repeat some of the steps. Ask and answer as many critical and relevant questions as you can.

Step 1: Look.

What do I see? Look at the image and articulate what is going on.

1. What do you see in this image?
2. Are there people in the image? What are they doing? How are they presented?
3. What do you notice about the setting, place, or context?
4. What objects or components do you see?
5. How is the image composed? How are elements in the image arranged?
6. What colors are used in the image? What effects are created by the use of color?

Step 2: Read.

What does the text tell me? Read any textual information that accompanies the image and consider what else it tells you.

1. What text accompanies the image?
2. What is the purpose of the textual information?
3. What kind of context does the textual information provide?
4. Can you determine *where, how, why,* and *for whom* the image was made?

Step 3: Examine.

What do I see now? Now that you know more, examine the image again.

1. What do you see now that you didn't see before?
2. Did reading the text change how you see the image? How?
3. What are the most important visual elements in the image? How can you tell?
4. Can you interpret the image in different ways?

Step 4: Describe.

What does this mean? Describe the image and its subject.

1. What meanings are conveyed by the information, people, things, or actions in the image?
2. How do design choices contribute to the meaning of the image?
3. Why might the image have been created, and who might have been the intended audience?
4.. How does this image function? Does it illustrate, document, entertain, persuade, and so on?
5. How was the image made?
6. If you were asked what the image is "about," what subjects would you describe?

Step 5: Check understanding.

What else do I need to know? Generate new questions based on your findings.

1. What do you need to find out more about?
2. How does the image fit with or disrupt what you already know?
3. How does your interpretation align with or differ from that of others?
4. How might discipline-specific or interdisciplinary perspectives or approaches further inform your analysis?

Reflect.

Scan your answers to the preceding questions. What will your next step be?

Analyzing an Ad for Context

LEARNING OUTCOME

- Analyze an advertisement for social and historical context.

DESCRIPTION

This activity takes students through the process of critically analyzing an advertisement. Distribute the **Analyzing an Ad for Context Worksheet** and have students work through the questions individually or in pairs or groups. The worksheet ends by asking students to list several sources for finding information about the social and historical context of the ad. Grappling with the questions in this activity helps students to see everyday images as cultural artifacts, enhancing their visual and information literacy skills at the same time.

TIPS FOR SUCCESS

- Provide students with a historical advertisement from a time period they are studying.
- Once you choose an ad for this activity, be sure that you know the answer to the final question; moving students from examining an ad to locating appropriate background sources makes this activity work in library instruction.

OPTIONAL EXTENSIONS

- Choose a current ad for the same (or similar) product and go through the activity questions again. Discuss similarities and differences.
- Instruct students to write descriptions of the people or objects in the image, including such aspects as physical features, facial expressions, clothes, hair, gestures, colors, textures, and so on.
- Show students an image, then ask them to play the part of a news reporter preparing to write a story about an event depicted in the image. Students record the details of the event in a notebook and share their thoughts with the class.

VISUAL LITERACY STANDARDS CONNECTION

- ACRL Visual Literacy Standard 3, Performance Indicators 1–4
- ACRL Visual Literacy Standard 4, Performance Indicators 1–3

Analyzing an Ad for Context

Look at the advertisement and answer the following questions.

1. Where does your eye go? Why?
   _____
   _____

2. What is the relationship between the text and the image?
   _____
   _____

3. What ambience or mood does this ad create?
   _____
   _____

4. What might it have been like to see this ad when it came out?
   _____
   _____

5. What does this ad tell you about the ideal (look, role, relationship, etc.) of the time?
   _____
   _____

6. What role do you think this product played in the culture and society in which it was created?
   _____
   _____

7. What sociological, political, economic, or cultural attitudes are reflected in this ad?
   _____
   _____

8. Where could you go to learn more about this ad's time period? List *at least* three source ideas.
   _____
   _____

Analyzing an Ad for Context

This Pepsi-Cola ad was used in a library research workshop for a food-writing course at New York University during former mayor Bloomberg's attempt to ban large sugary drinks in New York City. Students analyzed the following ad, scanned from the *New York Times*. This full-page ad appeared on February 12, 1956, on page SM133, adjacent to an article called "Pizza a la mode: In many variations, Italy's famous pie now rivals the hot dog in popularity." The ad positions Pepsi as a beverage with health benefits. The copy leads with "How come this brimming land of plenty should produce the leanest, fittest-looking men and slimmest-waisted women in the world?" and ends with "Have a Pepsi—the modern, light refreshment." (Continued on page 25)

Pepsi Ad scanned from the New York Times *(February 12, 1956, p. SM133)*

Analyzing an Ad for Context (continued)

Look at the advertisement and answer the following questions.

1. Where does your eye go? Why?

   My eye goes right to the couple's heads, probably because the picture is composed to draw you in and want to know more about them.

2. What is the relationship between the text and the image?

   The image is the main focus and then the text supports what's presented—the couple is really good looking, and the text says that Pepsi goes along with a "sensible trend in diet."

3. What ambience or mood does this ad create?

   The mood is sort of romantic and classy, in an old-fashioned and traditional way.

4. What might it have been like to see this ad when it came out?

   It might make you feel bad about yourself if you're not as well-dressed as the couple!

5. What does this ad tell you about the ideal (look, role, relationship, etc.) of the time?

   It seems like people really paid attention to their outfits—the woman is wearing a hat and gloves.

6. What role do you think this product played in the culture and society in which it was created?

   They're calling it a "modern, light, refreshment" and they have it set up almost like a cocktail.

7. What sociological, political, economic, or cultural attitudes are reflected in this ad?

   For starters, the couple is white and heterosexual—pretty old school. The text says that Americans "keep slender and fit through their wholesome, up-to-date eating habits," so it seems like being skinny was a social pressure then, just like today!

8. Where could you go to learn more about this ad's time period? List at least three source ideas.

   I could ask my grandmother because she was alive in the 1950s or try to find a book about the history of soda; maybe news stories written during the 1950s would be good too.

Comparing Image Metadata

LEARNING OUTCOMES

- Compare image metadata from different sources.
- Practice reading metadata to understand images.

DESCRIPTION

Students compare metadata accompanying images from different sources and become familiar with the types of information included in image metadata. As students work with a partner to find two images related to a topic, you provide guidance by suggesting image databases or sources relevant to the course and student topics. Students then analyze each image's metadata and complete the **Comparing Image Metadata Worksheet**. Use the suggested prompts to discuss findings.

DISCUSSION PROMPTS

- Which source provided the most metadata with the image?
- Were any of the metadata labels confusing (e.g., medium, repository, etc.)?
- What kinds of metadata did you find most useful for understanding the image (e.g., title, date, tags, etc.)?
- Was there information you expected to find about an image that wasn't there?

TIP FOR SUCCESS

- Find image sources for this activity in advance and provide an easy way for students to connect to those sources, such as by providing links on a course guide.

VISUAL LITERACY STANDARDS CONNECTION

- ACRL Visual Literacy Standard 2, Performance Indicator 2
- ACRL Visual Literacy Standard 3, Performance Indicators 1, 2, and 4

Comparing Image Metadata

In the following chart, record the metadata you find with each of two images.

	IMAGE FROM SOURCE 1	IMAGE FROM SOURCE 2
Database or source		
Title		
Creator		
Date of creation		
Image size		
How was the image created?		
Are any tags or keywords attached to the image?		
Is there a caption or other description?		
What other metadata are included?		

Evaluating Data Visualizations in the News

LEARNING OUTCOMES

- Interpret data and information displayed in charts and graphs.
- Consider alternative formats for data visualization.
- Evaluate the effectiveness of charts and graphs for purpose and argument.

DESCRIPTION

This activity provides a scaffolded process for interpreting and evaluating graphs that display information from the same data set. Students begin by reading a news article that presents an argument using graphs, then complete the **Evaluating Data Visualizations in the News Worksheet** comparing several graphs.

For this activity we use a February 7, 2015, online article in *Vox*, "Master's Degrees Are as Common Now as Bachelor's Degrees Were in the '60s," which claims that "the master's degree is the fastest-growing college credential in the US," and explore the source data sets from the National Center for Education Statistics.

First, students describe what they see in graph 1 (the first graph contained in the article) and then compare it to graph 2 (an alternative graph created in Excel using additional information from the article's source data set, available at nces.ed.gov/programs/digest/d13/tables/dt13_318.20.asp). Discuss which graph is better at conveying the information clearly and effectively. Next, students compare graph 2 and graph 3, which demonstrate that different graph formats can offer different, legitimate ways of presenting data. Finally, students compare graphs 4 and 5 with the previous graphs to explore how other authoritative methods are used to communicate these data. Students write or discuss their answers to the questions in the activity and reflect on which data and graphs they might include if tasked with writing a piece about the same issue.

DISCUSSION PROMPTS

When comparing graphs 1 and 2:

- Do you notice any elements that are missing from graph 1?
  Note: Graph 1 is missing several important elements—it lacks a complete title, a *y*-axis label, and a proper source citation.
- Do you notice anything questionable about the data?
  Note: Along the *x*-axis in graph 1 (years), the interval between data points jumps from data points every ten years to annually; however, the data points themselves are graphed at a uniform interval. This changes the shape of the line and therefore the effectiveness of the claim.

- What additional data does graph 2 include? What role do these data play?

  Note: Graph 2 includes an additional series—the number of bachelor's degrees. This provides more context, to be more consistent with the original claim. After all, the title of the news piece begs a comparison between master's and bachelor's degrees.

When comparing graphs 2 and 3:

- What differences do you notice between graphs 2 and 3?

  Note: Here the data points are the same, but by using a different type of graph (a stacked bar chart instead of a line graph) we see different aspects of the data more effectively and ask more questions. Although the original line graph can show the total number and trend for bachelor's and master's degrees, the strength of the stacked bar chart is that it can more readily show the proportion and changing proportions over time. At the same time the stacked bar chart has a drawback in that it doesn't show the total number of bachelor's degrees as clearly.

When comparing graphs 4 and 5 with the previous graphs:

- How are these graphs different from those seen earlier?

  Note: It is important to consider additional sources of information and visualizations to understand an issue. Graph 4 is an example of how the pros do it. By examining an authoritative source, students may see how others communicate and think about different types of data or topics. In graph 4, from the February 2012 U.S. Census Bureau Report, "Educational Attainment in the United States: 2009," the data are presented as the proportion of the population with a given educational attainment; in other words, this graph is corrected for the natural population growth of U.S. college-age students across the decades. Graph 5 adapts the visualization approach from the U.S. Census, with the addition of master's degree data, and a different view of the data emerges than originally presented in graph 1.

- Do these graphs help you understand the topic?

  Note: In some cases exploring the underlying data set can reveal different stories than originally presented. Data visualizations should be tools for thinking clearly about a topic. Seeking additional information (e.g., controlling for natural population growth) can be important to communicating the full story within the data.

TIPS FOR SUCCESS

- Use the "Visualizing Data" section of this chapter to discuss the common purposes for different types of charts and graphs. Depending on the context, there is not always a right or wrong answer. Students will begin to assess the strengths and weaknesses of different types of graphs, as well as the way data visualizations are used to make an argument.

- When selecting graphs to use with your students, consider the following:
    ◊ Are the design and function of excellent or poor quality?
    ◊ Are the sources and methods of the data clear from the visualization and reliable?
    ◊ Is the chart or graph engaging enough to lead to interesting questions?

OPTIONAL EXTENSIONS
- Expand the discussion to analyze the article's specific claims and whether the graphs help support these claims and provide a clear understanding of the issue. Give your students the opportunity to explore the data set and additional visualizations to see what other stories the data might be telling.
- Have students create different types of charts and graphs with Excel using the same data set from the National Center for Educational Statistics.

VISUAL LITERACY STANDARDS CONNECTION
- ACRL Visual Literacy Standard 4, Performance Indicator 1
- ACRL Visual Literacy Standard 6, Performance Indicator 1

Evaluating Data Visualizations in the News

As you examine each graph, describe what you see and what you think the graph means.

Step 1: Describe what you see in graph 1.

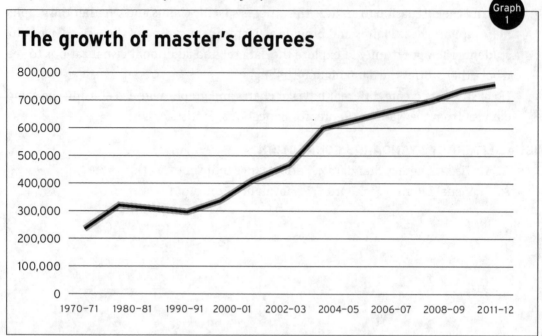

Graph 1

The growth of master's degrees

Source: Education Department

1. What information is this graph presenting? _____
   _____

2. What are the components or variables? _____
   _____

3. What are the units of measure? _____

4. What is the source of the data? _____
   _____

5. Can you name the type of graph? _____

6. Why would you use this type of graph? _____
   _____

7. Do you think this is an effective graph? _____
   Why or why not? _____
   _____

With contribution from Russ White.

Step 2: Compare graphs 1 and 2.

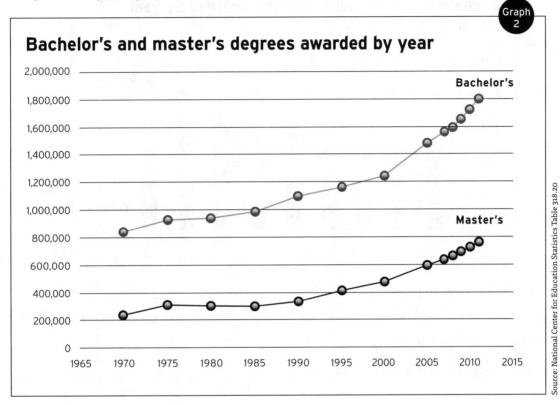

Graph 2

Bachelor's and master's degrees awarded by year

Bachelor's

Master's

Source: National Center for Education Statistics Table 318.20

8. What's different in graph 2? _____
   _____

9. Does graph 2 improve understanding of the data and overall topic? Why or why not? _____
   _____

10. Does graph 2 strengthen or weaken the original written argument? _____
    _____

Step 3: Compare graphs 2 and 3.

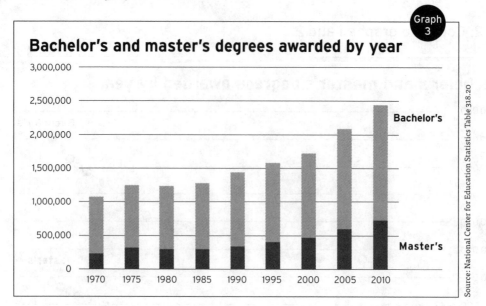

Bachelor's and master's degrees awarded by year

Graph 3

Bachelor's

Master's

Source: National Center for Education Statistics Table 318.20

11. What's different compared to graph 2? _____

_____

12. Can you name the type of graph? _____

13. Why would you use this type of graph? _____

_____

14. Is graph 3 more or less effective than graph 2? _____

_____

Step 4: Compare graphs 4 and 5 with the previous graphs.

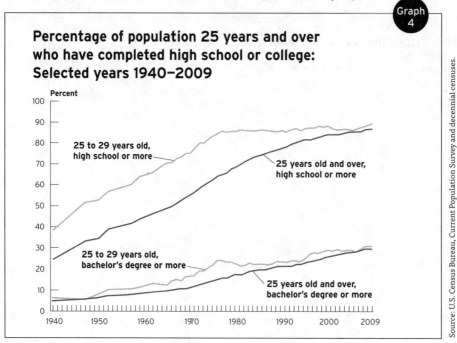

Graph 4

Percentage of population 25 years and over who have completed high school or college: Selected years 1940–2009

Percent

25 to 29 years old, high school or more

25 years old and over, high school or more

25 to 29 years old, bachelor's degree or more

25 years old and over, bachelor's degree or more

Source: U.S. Census Bureau, Current Population Survey and decennial censuses.

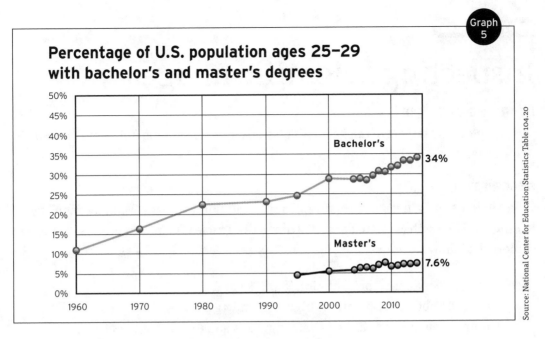

Percentage of U.S. population ages 25–29
with bachelor's and master's degrees

Bachelor's — 34%

Master's — 7.6%

1960 1970 1980 1990 2000 2010

Source: National Center for Education Statistics Table 104.20

Graph 5

15. How are graphs 4 and 5 different from the previous graphs? _____
_____

16. Do graphs 4 and 5 improve understanding of the data and overall topic? Why or why not? _____
_____

17. Do graphs 4 and 5 strengthen or weaken the original written argument? _____
_____

Step 5: Reflect.

If you were writing an article about trends in bachelor's and master's degrees, which graph(s) would
you include? _____
_____

Inspecting Scientific Images

LEARNING OUTCOME

- Explore the impact of image manipulations in the production of scientific knowledge.

DESCRIPTION

Lead students to "What's in a Picture? The Temptation of Image Manipulation" by Mike Rossner and Kenneth M. Yamada, or distribute the article. Then form groups of students to explore the following issues:

- Group A: Gross misrepresentation (figures 1 and 2)
- Group B: Subtle manipulations (figures 3 and 4)
- Group C: Misrepresentation of data (figures 5 and 6)

After students complete the **Inspecting Scientific Images Worksheet**, use the PowerPoint slides provided with the article (http://jcb.rupress.org/content/166/1/11.full) as prompts for each group to discuss the examples of manipulations in scientific images.

DISCUSSION PROMPTS

Each group chooses one issue and a consequence to present to the class. Additional prompts include the following:

- Why did you choose the issue you did?
- What does image manipulation mean for you as a reader of scientific literature?
- What does image manipulation mean for you as a potential author?

TIPS FOR SUCCESS

- Before conducting this activity, gain an understanding of image manipulation in the sciences by reading the following articles:
  - ◊ Mike Rossner and Kenneth M. Yamada (2004), "What's in a Picture? The Temptation of Image Manipulation," *Journal of Cell Biology* 166 (1): 11–15, http://jcb.rupress.org/content/166/1/11.full.
  - ◊ Mike Blatt and Cathie Martin (2013), "Manipulation and Misconduct in the Handling of Image Data," *Plant Physiology* 163 (1): 3–4, www.plantphysiol.org/content/163/1/3.short.
- If your class is large, assign two groups to each issue.

OPTIONAL EXTENSIONS

- Many open-access scientific journals allow readers to download the images. Ask students to download the image from a PLOS (Public Library of Science) article, apply a change to the image, and then describe how the change might impact a researcher's interpretation of the image.
- The PLOS guide to figures (http://journals.plos.org/plosbiology/s/figures) pairs well with this activity.
- Expand this activity with the Council of Science Editors' "White Paper on Publication Ethics" (www.councilscienceeditors.org/resource-library/editorial-policies/white-paper-on-publication-ethics). Section 3.4, *Digital Images and Misconduct,* contains guidelines for handling image data and suggested procedures for dealing with violations of the guidelines.
- Shift the focus to image analysis and use NASA's tips and strategies (http://earthobservatory.nasa.gov/Features/ColorImage) for reading satellite images.

VISUAL LITERACY STANDARDS CONNECTION

- ACRL Visual Literacy Standard 2, Performance Indicator 2
- ACRL Visual Literacy Standard 3, Performance Indicators 1, 2, and 4

Inspecting Scientific Images

Complete the steps using the article "What's in a Picture? The Temptation of Image Manipulation" by Mike Rossner and Kenneth M. Yamada.

Circle your group.

   a. Gross misrepresentation (figures 1 and 2)
   b. Subtle manipulations (figures 3 and 4)
   c. Misrepresentation of data (figures 5 and 6)

Step 1: Examine your assigned figures and read the accompanying section of the article, then complete the table.

LIST ISSUES PRESENTED IN THIS SECTION	DESCRIBE A CONSEQUENCE OF EACH ISSUE

Step 2: Choose one issue and a consequence to present to the class. Be prepared to answer the following questions:

   1. Describe the image manipulation issue and the consequence.
   2. Explain how what you learned about image manipulation will inform the way you interpret and analyze scientific images in the future.

Find the Right Images

FINDING JUST THE right image can seem daunting. You may be able to visualize exactly what you're looking for, but how do you translate that mental picture into an actual image that you can use? Maybe you've come across an image that communicates what you're trying to say, but you're not sure whether it's available for the kind of use you have in mind. It can be difficult to know where to look for images and how to navigate the millions of choices available. The resources, strategies, and activities in this chapter will build your repertoire of approaches to finding images and guiding students as they look for images.

Finding images is not as simple as knowing where to look. Like all research, it is an iterative process that involves multimodal exploration, browsing, learning more, and then exploring further. There may be times when you are looking for a specific image, with an established title and creator. But more often, visual content is not easily defined by words. This chapter reveals sources and search strategies for finding the images you need.

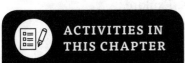

Foundational Questions

What Kind of Image Do I Need?

Before starting your image search, take a moment to reflect. Think about how your image needs to look, what it will communicate, and how you plan to use it. What purpose does the image serve in your overall project? What are some words that might describe the image? Next, think about your planned image use—are there any constraints associated with it?

Where Do I Look First?

Use our guides to types of image sources to better understand your options. Do you need an image for your blog or research guide? You'll need an image available for use on the open web, so consider Creative Commons or open media. For academic projects, image research typically is most effective when conducted in conjunction with textual research. Maybe the image you need is in one of the articles on your topic or on a website you're already consulting.

What Search Strategies Will I Use?

Update your image search strategies. Finding images differs in a few important ways from finding textual materials, so you'll want to experiment with different approaches to discover which ones work best for you. As you work with different types of images and sources, keep track of your favorite strategies, keywords, and sources.

Do I Need to Try More Sources or Strategies?

If you reach a dead end in your image search, try new types of sources, use different keywords, or try browsing instead of searching. Are there blogs or websites that use images you like? Follow the image links for source ideas. Notice the tags and keywords used to describe the kinds of images you're looking for, and incorporate them into your searches. Find out more about your topic generally, and this research will open up new ideas for finding images. Explore color-search, reverse image search, and other tools to expand your options.

How Do I Keep Track of What Works?

When you want to use the images you've found, whether for study or new creative projects, you'll need to know where the images came from, information about them, and how to cite them. Set up a system for tracking images and their information that is easy to use, and use it consistently. You'll be glad you did as you progress with your image searches and projects.

Before You Search

Before you start looking for an image, take some time to think about the kind of image content you need and how you plan to use it. This preliminary work helps you determine where to look for images and sets you up for an efficient search. You will save yourself research time and frustration by avoiding common image-research pitfalls, such as finding the perfect image only to determine it is restricted and not available for the reuse you have planned.

A good first step is to visualize the image you'd like to find and jot down words that describe it. You are accustomed to generating keywords for text-based research, and this practice is an extension of that process. It requires an additional step: translating what you are visualizing into words you can use to search. Think about things, places, and people that might be featured in the image you need. What kind of action or event is pictured? Are there certain colors you're looking for? Would you like the image to evoke a particular feeling or reaction? If you're looking for a specific image, write down everything you know about it, including artist or photographer, date, location, title words. This process of articulating with words what you're looking for in visual content moves your image research forward. Add synonyms, variations, and other words that might come to mind, and update your keyword list as you discover how images are described in different sources.

Next, let your planned use for the image guide where you start your search. If you're looking for an image to post on a website or to reuse in a creative project, avoid restricted databases or sources that make images available for viewing only. Sources we list in this chapter as "open" are ideal for this type of project. Library subscription image databases, on the other hand, are useful for high-quality teaching and educational-use images for study and academic projects. As with any research, be prepared to consult multiple sources.

Make note of any technical requirements you may have for the image. Does it need to be screen-sized or larger for a presentation? Or do you just need a small image to refer to in a paper? **Activity 2.1: Preparing for Image Searching** will help you and your students lay the groundwork for an efficient and effective image search.

Image Sources

At some point, you've likely experienced a moment of hesitation when asked to help a student find an image for a project: Where should you start? Or maybe you're working on a presentation of your own and want to include images but suspect you're overlooking something. You've also likely faced moments of frustration after finding an image you'd like to use, only to discover that it is restricted or not available for reuse.

Take some time to familiarize yourself with the image sources we've included here, and you'll soon develop a list of your personal favorites. You'll find sources ideal for your students and their research and for your own professional use. Use **Activity 2.2: Exploring Digital Image Sources** to delve into a variety of image sources and discover new options for finding images.

In the section that follows, we've noted which sources include open, restricted, or a mixture of image content. If you're looking for images you need to reuse in an open environment, you can save yourself time by skipping restricted image sources and going right to the ones with content available for reuse. Many sources contain both open image content and restricted image content, so be sure to double-check any licenses or restrictions on individual images within these sources. **Activity 2.3: Finding Creative Commons Images** explores locating and examining Creative Commons images.

TYPES OF IMAGE SOURCES

Knowing a little bit about different types of image sources means you'll know where to look for the images you need when you need them. Explore must-know information about the following image source types and our **Top Picks** in each category. Refer to the icons in the **Image Rights and Availability** key to determine the typical image usage rights and availability for each image source.

- Image search engines
- Image sharing sites
- Social media sites
- Government image sources
- Stock image websites
- Museum, archive, and library digital collections
- Library databases and discovery systems

Discover additional image sources and stay up-to-date with **More to Explore: Guides to Image Resources** later in this chapter.

Image Search Engines

Image-specific search engines, such as Google Images, are not image sources per se. Rather, they help you to find images on websites, blogs, and other Internet sites. Image search engines retrieve images by matching your search terms to website text. This text, which is on the same page as the image or in the website metadata, may not specifically describe the image. Some image search engines have reverse image search features that use image-based algorithms to find matching or similar images. Drop an image into the search box instead of entering keywords, and the search engine will find that image wherever it appears on the Internet. Image search engines are great for obtaining a quick visual identification, generating new ideas for research,

Key: Image Rights and Availability

- ⊙ = open image content
- 🔒 = restricted image content
- ㏄ = Creative Commons-licensed images
- ⌁ = share, link, or embed images
- 👤 = login required
- $ = includes pay-per-image options

Top Picks: Image Search Engines

Google Images

The go-to image search engine. Advanced search features useful for filtering results by size, type, color, date, rights, and more. Drop image into search box for reverse image search.

Bing Images

The image search defaults to show "popular searches," so can help uncover trending topics. The Image Match feature can uncover web pages that include a specific image.

TinEye Reverse Image Search

Reverse image search tool. Use in addition to Google Images to locate other instances of an image online.

finding multiple sources for images, figuring out where an image came from, and finding Creative Commons images from a wide variety of sources.

Image Sharing Sites

Members generate the content in image sharing sites. The quality of the content and the information that accompanies the images is entirely dependent upon contributors and ranges from minimal to extensive. The rights that contributors assert over the content they contribute also varies. Many sites

Top Picks: Image Sharing Sites

Flickr

The dominant image sharing site, containing millions of images. Especially strong content in areas of photography, travel, architecture, and the built environment. Use the Advanced Search to limit results to Creative Commons content.

Flickr's The Commons

A subset of Flickr images. Content contributed by cultural institutions around the world, including libraries and museums. Includes primarily historical, public domain, and "no known copyright" material.

Multicolr Search Lab powered by TinEye

Flickr search overlay that discovers Flickr Creative Commons content based on color. Select colors on palette, adjust color ratio, and add tags to limit search.

Wikimedia Commons

Images contributed by the public. Contains public domain, open, and Creative Commons images.

COFFEE BREAK!

Reverse Image Searching

1. Choose an image and perform a reverse image search with TinEye.
2. Using the same image, try a reverse image search using Google Images.
3. Compare the results.

REFLECT

How might you use these tools in your work?

let you limit your search to images with a Creative Commons license. Navigate by license to ensure you're only searching images available for the use you have in mind. Specialized tools have emerged to aid in image discovery on sharing sites, based on license, color, or other factors. Some image sharing sites include content contributed by libraries, museums, and archives, so there is some overlap with these institutional sources. Image sharing sites are best used for photography, visual communication, and illustration.

Social Media Sites

Your students may share images and video on one or more social media platforms such as Facebook or Instagram, making these platforms a familiar reference point for explaining how other image sites work. Explore social media sites to generate ideas for research, especially for current and pop-culture topics. Social media sites usually require a login for full access to content, and linking and reposting, rather than downloading and repurposing, are the norm.

Top Picks: Social Media Sites

Instagram
Social networking site built for sharing photos and short videos. Requires login to view photos.

Pinterest
Visual sharing site where users pin bookmarks of images and web content to boards. Requires login to view pins.

Top Picks: Government Image Sources

USA.gov
Search U.S. government content, then limit to images.

NASA Images
Images from NASA, including still and video.

National Park Service Digital Image Archives
Contemporary photography and historical collections. Images of national parks, monuments, battlefields, historic sites, and more.

U.S. Department of Agriculture Image Gallery
Food, plants, animals, insects, and other agriculture-related images.

U.S. Fish and Wildlife Service: National Digital Library
Photos, artifacts, and media from the Fish and Wildlife Service.

Government Image Sources

U.S. government agencies make the images they produce available to the public through the agencies' websites. These images are typically created for documentary, educational, informational, scientific, or communication purposes. Most of these images contain public government information and are free for you to use for any purpose. There are exceptions, however, so look for rights statements and disclaimers about copyright status. Distinguish images *produced* by the government from images *held* by government institutions. For example, the U.S. government did not produce most images in the Smithsonian Institution databases, which are images of items in the institution's collections and may be restricted. Images produced by state and local governments, as well as by many foreign governments, may also be protected by copyright. Find government images online by limiting your search to the domain .gov.

Stock Image Websites

Stock image websites include photographs taken by professional or contributing photographers, artists, or designers. Most stock image sites have a fee structure for different types of uses and offer some content without charge for general purposes. Getty Images, for example, allows anyone to use some of its images online by embedding the images with a link back to the site. Try a reverse image search on the stock image you've selected to see how others have

Top Picks: Stock Image Websites

Getty Images
Many images include code for embedding directly into blogs and websites, with accompanying credit line. Fees for most other uses.

Morguefile
Free, high-resolution, digital stock photography contributed by participating photographers and creatives. Great for presentations.

The Noun Project
Icons, symbols, and graphics for visual communication. Join and sign in to download icons for free.

used it, especially if you're aiming for a unique look. Stock image websites are useful for linked images on websites or blogs, for illustrations, and for visual communication.

Museum, Archive, and Library Digital Collections

Many museums, archives, and libraries have online digital collections representing materials in their physical collections. Images may include works of art, artifacts, special collections materials, local history items, and photographs. Images are typically high-quality reproductions taken directly from the originals (or are born-digital originals) and are often accompanied by reliable and in-depth information. Online exhibits help users browse relevant images. Look for open access content; many institutions are making some or all of their images available without restrictions. Museum, archive, and library collections are ideal for academic research and for exploring potential primary source materials.

Library Databases and Discovery Systems

Libraries subscribe to databases, and many contain image content designed specifically for research and academic use. Some databases include only images, and others include images with text. Typically, licensed databases have restrictions on how you can use the images in them. Most do not permit posting their images on the open web but do allow use in presentations, papers, or other projects that will have a limited audience at your institution. Some library discovery systems, such as WorldCat and Primo, index image databases and possibly your institution's digital collections or local image databases. A

Top Picks: Museum, Archive, and Library Digital Collections

Digital Public Library of America

Discovery tool that retrieves materials from library, archive, and museum digital collections. Exhibits are based on topics and themes. Check rights statements for individual images.

Europeana

Cultural heritage portal with images contributed by European museums, libraries, and archives. Rights are clearly indicated and vary by contributor.

World Digital Library

This project of the Library of Congress, with the support of UNESCO and partners from around the world, aims to make multilingual primary source materials freely available.

Library of Congress: American Memory

A "digital record of American history and creativity," including still and moving images, prints, maps, and more. Items from the Library of Congress and other contributing institutions.

Library of Congress: Prints and Photographs Online Catalog

Pictures in the Library of Congress's holdings. Includes photographs, prints, drawings, posters, architectural drawings, and other still images.

National Gallery of Art: NGA Images

Open access digital images of the collections of the National Gallery of Art (U.S.).

NYPL Digital Gallery

Illuminated manuscripts, historical maps, vintage posters, rare prints, photographs, and more from the New York Public Library. Free medium-sized image download, purchase large-sized.

U.S. National Library of Medicine: Images from the History of Medicine

Includes portraits, photographs, and art illustrating all aspects of medicine from the fifteenth to twenty-first centuries.

discovery system can be an efficient and powerful tool for conducting image and text research concurrently. Determine how your library discovery system treats image content and what sources it indexes; then be sure to explore terms of use provided by each source.

> ## Top Picks: Library Databases and Discovery Systems
>
> ### Artstor 🔒
> Images from museum collections and special contributors across the disciplines. Advanced features allow you to limit by geography, material type, culture, style, and more. Most images can be used for educational purposes only—IAP (Images for Academic Publishing) are an exception.
>
> ### AP Images 🔒
> Photographs, audio, and graphics from the Associated Press. Photographs date back to the 1800s and go up to the present date.
>
> ### Library Catalogs 🔓🔒
> Some library catalogs index image databases, such as Artstor, and library digital collections. Explore your library's discovery system to see how it handles image and media content.

Image Search Strategies

Much of what you already know about search strategies translates to searching for images, but there are some specific tips, tricks, and approaches to keep in mind when looking for visual materials. To find images, it is important to understand how images are typically described, how search engines and databases retrieve images, and the limitations of different types of sources.

Images are retrieved through searching the text that accompanies them, including captions, titles, tags, descriptions, surrounding text, the web page that the image is embedded in, html markup, and other types of metadata. Images are typically not cataloged with controlled vocabularies the way books are. The text that does accompany an image is usually general topical text. Visual components and subjects of images are rarely described in detail. Features we rely on to retrieve text materials, such as full-text searches, are not available with visuals. Finding images in this environment becomes challenging when textual elements are missing or lacking in quality, or when the words used to search for an image do not match the words that accompany the image. **Activity 2.4: Understanding Image Descriptions for Smarter Searching** delves into the role of text in image discovery.

Image-specific search tools provide expanded and unique options for discovering visual materials. There are times when a visual search is the only way to access color or other image specifications and design features. For example, imagine that you are looking for a photo of a green landscape. Google Images can retrieve images by color through its combined application of text and visual search algorithms. Flickr would be another good bet for this type of search because it employs user-generated tags and descriptions that often capture color or design elements. In contrast, library databases typically include context-based information about images alongside text-only retrieval options, so searching for attributes such as an image's color will get you nowhere. Students' search experiences with library databases will be entirely different from their experiences with image search engines or image sharing sites, and you'll want to expose them to multiple approaches to finding images. Use **Activity 2.5: Reverse Image Searching** to practice visual search strategies and to analyze how advanced visual search functions can be useful for research.

Keep the scope of different types of search engines and sources in mind. Internet image search engines do not index all images on the Web. Digital image collections provided by libraries, archives, museums, galleries, and stock photo sites, for example, are often hidden because search engine crawlers cannot retrieve content within databases. These databases have to be consulted individually or accessed by way of alternative indexing systems, such as library discovery platforms, or portals such as the Digital Public Library of America.

Remember, too, that not all visual content is available digitally or online. Particularly with specialized research, you may need to consult institutional archives, special collections, books, or other print sources. Your library's print collections can offer millions of quality visual materials, ranging from art reproductions to maps, drawings, and photography. To find books with image content, try searching for a topic and adding "ill." or "illus." These abbreviations are often included as part of the physical description of the book in the catalog record. Another trick of the trade is to use the Library of Congress Subject Heading "Pictorial Works." You can deploy these strategies when searching large corpuses of digitized print books that use subject indexing, such as HathiTrust, and for smarter searching in tools such as Google Books.

Keeping Track of What You Find

Tracking your image research provides big payoffs down the road. Maybe you've been in this situation: You have an image on your desktop that you saved a long time ago and now you want to include it in a new presentation, but you're having difficulty citing it because you can't remember who the creator

Image Search Principles

Keep these principles in mind to find the right image.

CONSIDER RIGHTS ISSUES

Before you start to search, think about how you'll be using the images and whether you'll need Creative Commons or open usage rights. If so, you'll want to search sources with open content first.

ENGAGE IN "PRE-SEARCH"

Do some exploratory searching to familiarize yourself with the search features—use filters, facets, and advanced search features wherever possible. Recognize that text and images often appear together, so text sources are a great way to discover images. Use reference and topical sources to generate lists of images to find.

READ THE TEXT

Descriptions and metadata that accompany images are essential for searching and finding images. Be mindful of the role that text plays in connecting you with visual content to improve your search results.

START SMALL

You may be accustomed to finding articles by entering a full citation into a search engine and going directly to the item you need. This strategy does not work with images. Start with one or two keywords, and narrow and filter from there.

USE LATERAL THINKING

Consider individual, company, organizational websites as well as specialty blogs or news sites that cover your topic. Uncover images by adding "archive," "database," or "gallery" to a topical web search, then search the archive or image database itself to find the images you're looking for. Use reverse image searching to find other instances of an image online.

KEEP TRACK OF SUCCESSES

Did you find the perfect source for images in your discipline? Maybe you found a handful of images that will be perfect for your next presentation. Whatever the case, make a note of it. Keep track of useful images, sources, and the information you'll need for citations. When you come back to images later, you'll be glad you recorded the essential information about them.

is, what it's called, or even where you found it. Avoid these problems and save yourself time by designating a system and place to save images and accompanying information *as you find them.*

Use tools that are already part of your everyday workflows, and encourage students to do the same. Are you or your students always on Google? Use Drive to save a folder of images and a doc to track the information and links. Do you use Pinterest regularly? Set up a space just for your work- and image-related pictures and links. Or try using Padlet to drop in images as you find them— they'll be available for later reuse with a link; there's no need to download the image and transcribe the information separately.

Create a running list of image sources that consistently yield useful results for your purposes. If Wikimedia Commons comes through for you every time, keep that information handy. When students need contemporary art inspiration for creative projects and you notice that Artsy helps, add it to your research guide. Maybe you're working with nursing students, and you see that they gravitate toward the medical history galleries of Wellcome Images; you want

COFFEE BREAK!

Image Storage Practices

Take a quick inventory of how and where you store images and information.

List all the locations where you currently keep images:

_____   _____   _____

_____   _____   _____

_____   _____   _____

Do you have a system for keeping track of images?

What about image information? If you wanted to reuse an image, can you quickly access rights and citation information?

Identify two tools you use every day.

Would either of these tools help you streamline your image and information storage?

to make sure you can point next year's students to the same resources. Having a system for remembering the best sources for your students and for your own projects ensures that you'll easily find new images the next time.

Whatever your system, use it consistently. Image content can be integrated into every aspect of scholarly work and intellectual life. Getting a handle on the proliferation of choices and possibilities brings you closer to a productive use of images, and streamlining your processes makes your use of visual content that much easier. If all else fails and you've lost track of an image, try tracking it down with a reverse image search.

Next Steps

Image research is not a single-search-then-find process. Rather, it is an iterative process integral to academic research and knowledge production. To move forward with finding images, try the following:

- Take the time to plan your next image search and keep track of your results.
- Try a new search strategy, image source, or tool.
- Research the topic to generate more image ideas, and model this approach for students.

 MORE TO EXPLORE: GUIDES TO IMAGE RESOURCES

DIGITAL IMAGES COLLECTIONS GUIDE

ACRL's Image Resources Interest Group hosts this guide on ALA Connect. Image resources are organized by subject with a table of contents, and each source includes a link and description. Initially developed by Scott Spicer, University of Minnesota, and maintained by community members.

IMAGE SOURCES AND RIGHTS CLEARANCE AGENCIES

The College Art Association maintains this list of sources of art images for publication and teaching. Each source is accompanied by a description of its content and a summary of rights information.

OPENGLAM

The Open Knowledge Foundation's OpenGLAM initiative works to open access to cultural heritage. The initiative's monthly Curator's Choice series highlights open image content in institutions around the world.

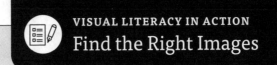
ACTIVITY 2.1

Preparing for Image Searching

LEARNING OUTCOMES

- Describe an image need and visualize possibilities.
- Translate visualization into words to prepare for image research.

DESCRIPTION

Get students ready to search for images by providing a few prompts to generate keywords. Students think about how an image needs to look, what it needs to communicate, how it will be used, and what purpose the image will serve in their overall project. Students also need to understand the difference between open and restricted images. This activity gets students in the habit of recording evolving search ideas as they find images.

TIP FOR SUCCESS

- Encourage students to think broadly about possible image content and to generate a variety of terms to describe what they are looking for. Considering people, actions, places, concepts, and color can help.

VISUAL LITERACY STANDARDS CONNECTION

- ACRL Visual Literacy Standard 1
- ACRL Visual Literacy Standard 2

Preparing for Image Searching

Complete the following activities *before* you search for an image. Organizing your thoughts and articulating what you are looking for saves time and frustration.

Describe the image you need, how you will use it, and what it might look like:

Do you need an open (unrestricted) image available for reuse?

Brainstorm a few descriptive words you might use for your image search:

As you search, capture new ideas for keywords and describe relevant images you find:

Preparing for Image Searching

Complete the following activities *before* you search for an image. Organizing your thoughts and articulating what you are looking for saves time and frustration.

Describe the image you need, how you will use it, and what it might look like:

I'm giving a presentation for my business class and need an image for risk-taking. I want it to show the benefits of risk-taking and forging a new path. I plan to post the presentation online and use it in my portfolio. I have an idea of a skier on a steep mountainside on a sunny day with ski tracks behind her.

Do you need an open (unrestricted) image available for reuse?

Yes, I plan to post this online and use it in my portfolio.

Brainstorm a few descriptive words you might use for your image search:

skier, skiing, powder, downhill, backcountry, extreme, mountain, recreation, risk

As you search, capture new ideas for keywords and describe relevant images you find:

I tried fly-in, resorts, ski guides, winter sports . . . and searched for "taking risks." Images of tightrope walking came up—they looked in line with the points I'm trying to make, so I started exploring them. I didn't want to use a generic image, so I did a new search to find good tightrope-walking images. I used the keywords tightrope, skyscraper, balancing, risk, chance.

Exploring Digital Image Sources

LEARNING OUTCOMES

- Describe features of online image sources.
- Consider the types of images available and the terms of use.

DESCRIPTION

Explore an image database such as Artstor or your library's digital collections. Use search, browse, and any online exhibit features to explore the kind of image content available. Point out where to find terms of use or license restrictions. Form groups and give each group an **Exploring Digital Image Sources Worksheet** along with one or two image sources from this chapter's "Image Sources" section to explore. Ask students to follow your example to find out about the source, the kinds of images it contains, and ways of finding those images. Students also try to find an image appropriate for the course or assignment as they explore the source. Students briefly share their image source with the class and fill out the rest of the worksheet as their peers share their assigned image sources.

TIPS FOR SUCCESS

- Ask students to think about search terms, browse functionality, image quality, metadata, scope, authority, provenance, and terms of use as they explore and compare image sources. This chapter's "Image Sources" section covers key characteristics to guide your discussion.
- If using Artstor, students will need to create personal logins to download and save images to groups. Once images are saved into a group, students can easily download the group of images into a PowerPoint file.

OPTIONAL EXTENSIONS

- Use the Artstor support materials (http://support.artstor.org). The Training and Finding sections are especially applicable.
- Instruct students to find and select three images that demonstrate different aspects, perspectives, or approaches to a theme or topic, then ask them to explain their choices to the class in person or by means of a course website.
- Use the activities in chapter 5, "Cite and Credit Images," to show students how to cite the images they find.

VISUAL LITERACY STANDARDS CONNECTION

- ACRL Visual Literacy Standard 1
- ACRL Visual Literacy Standard 2

Exploring Digital Image Sources

Step 1: Fill out the image source chart.

IMAGE SOURCE	TYPES OF IMAGES	SEARCH FEATURES OR CHALLENGES	TERMS OF USE OR LICENSE RESTRICTIONS

Step 2: Take note of specific images you found that are relevant to your assignment in this course.

Exploring Digital Image Sources

Step 1: Fill out the image source chart.

IMAGE SOURCE	TYPES OF IMAGES	SEARCH FEATURES OR CHALLENGES	TERMS OF USE OR LICENSE RESTRICTIONS
Google Images	Lots of images from the web.	It is easy to search! Can filter by size, color, rights.	Can be hard to find high-quality images and know where they come from.
Flickr	Mostly photos that people take and upload to the site. Lots of different subjects.	Explore categories, Camera finder, Galleries, Advanced Search. Many images to sort through to find what you need.	Anyone can post images here so not sure about how we can use them and cite them. Can limit to Creative Commons though.
Artstor	The images are high quality and have information about title, creator, etc.	The zoom feature shows details. Featured Groups were interesting, but not relevant to our topic. We had to try different terms to find images on our topic and didn't find that many. It took us a while to figure out how to download the image.	Looks like you can only use the images in the classroom and papers? That won't work for everything we want to do.

Step 2: Take note of specific images you found that are relevant to your assignment in this course.

Finding Creative Commons Images

LEARNING OUTCOMES

- Find images to reuse.
- Identify restrictions for image reuse.

DESCRIPTION

Begin by reviewing basic information about copyright and Creative Commons images. Review the four features, and accompanying symbols, that govern Creative Commons licenses (see chapter 4, "Ethical Use of Images"). Then show how to search for Creative Commons in Flickr by filtering to Creative Commons–licensed content. Point out where to locate the license associated with an image. Give students time to complete the **Finding Creative Commons Images Worksheet**, and discuss results.

TIPS FOR SUCCESS

- This activity can be conducted using a different image sharing site, such as Wikimedia Commons, or an image search engine, such as Google Images.
- Depending on the resource used, the background and search information will need to be adjusted accordingly (e.g., students may need to be able to identify public domain images).

OPTIONAL EXTENSIONS

- Ask students whether they would share (or have already shared) their own photographs under a Creative Commons license. If so, which license would they choose?
- In addition, you can show students ways to attach a Creative Commons license to their work in Flickr or another image sharing site.

VISUAL LITERACY STANDARDS CONNECTION

- ACRL Visual Literacy Standard 1, Performance Indicators 1 and 2
- ACRL Visual Literacy Standard 7, Performance Indicator 1

Finding Creative Commons Images

Search Flickr for a Creative Commons–licensed image. Capture as much information as you can about it.

Title: _____

Creator (real name, if available; Flickr username if not):

_____

URL: _____

Type of Creative Commons license: _____

In your own words, what does this license permit you to do with the image?

_____

_____

_____

_____

For what type of project can you imagine reusing this image?

_____

_____

_____

Finding Creative Commons Images

Search Flickr for a Creative Commons–licensed image. Capture as much information as you can about it.

Title: _Panda Bear at the ChongQing Zoo; Chongqing, China_

Creator (real name, if available; Flickr username if not):

atlassb

URL: _www.flickr.com/photos/atlastravelweb/3263611279_

Type of Creative Commons license: _Attribution-No Derivative_

In your own words, what does this license permit you to do with the image?

Share, but I have to follow the license terms, which say that

I have to give credit and indicate if I make changes to it.

If I build upon this image to create something new, I can't distribute it.

For what type of project can you imagine reusing this image?

This would be good for a presentation about pandas.

Understanding Image Descriptions for Smarter Searching

LEARNING OUTCOMES
- Recognize the role of textual information in providing access to image content.
- Identify types of textual information and metadata typically associated with images.

DESCRIPTION

Select an image that is described with subject terms or controlled vocabulary. Show the image to students without the metadata, then ask students to describe the image by writing all words that come to mind when they look at it, including not only what they see but also where the image is located, who created it, when it was made, and so forth. Students use the **Understanding Image Descriptions for Smarter Searching Worksheet** to compare their list with the subject terms and discuss differences and similarities in their descriptions. Then review the fundamentals of controlled vocabulary to illustrate why the keywords that students have generated may not match the controlled vocabularies used in the image database. If you're working with a database that uses a thesaurus or controlled vocabulary, show this to students so they can use this feature in other contexts. Note that most images are not fully cataloged with controlled vocabularies.

TIP FOR SUCCESS
- Use an image with rich metadata using controlled vocabularies, from a library digital collection or a subscription image database such as Artstor. Farm Security Administration/ Office of War Information (FSA-OWI) photographs from the Library of Congress also work well for this activity. Note that these images appear in different collections with varying levels of description, including many university library collections and Flickr.

OPTIONAL EXTENSIONS
- Repeat the activity with an image that has associated user-generated tags—use Flickr, Wikimedia, or another contribution-based image source. During discussion, emphasize that user-generated tags are a common feature of image description and require image researchers to search with synonyms, use multiple search terms, and deploy browse features.
- Incorporate Photogrammar, a free tool developed at Yale that uses Library of Congress FSA-OWI photograph metadata to provide expanded access points to this historical photograph collection. Note how metadata impact access to photographs by geographic location, photographer, date, or subject. Select a photograph to explore the metadata and the "similar photographs." How might these similarities be determined? Through metadata? A visual algorithm? Other ideas?

VISUAL LITERACY STANDARDS CONNECTION
- ACRL Visual Literacy Standard 2, Performance Indicator 2

Understanding Image Descriptions for Smarter Searching

Spend a few minutes looking at the image. Describe it by writing down as many words or phrases that come to mind:

_____

_____

_____

_____

How do your descriptive words compare to the terms used in the actual image description?

_____

_____

_____

_____

What is the role of the textual information (metadata) that accompanies the image?

_____

_____

_____

_____

How can you use what you've learned about image description to improve your future searches?

_____

_____

_____

_____

Reverse Image Searching

LEARNING OUTCOMES

- Practice reverse image searching.
- Consider potential applications for reverse image searching.

DESCRIPTION

Begin by demonstrating a visual search in Google Images. Point out key ways to view matching or "visually similar" images. In groups, students find an image related to the course content, then use that image to do a reverse image search using the **Reverse Image Searching Worksheet.** As a class, students share their findings and brainstorm potential uses for reverse image searching in their academic work. Use the discussion prompts to start the conversation and help students reflect.

DISCUSSION PROMPTS

- How might a reverse image search like the one you just did lead you to more information or ideas for research?
- In what other ways might an image search engine be useful to you in your academic work?

TIPS FOR SUCCESS

- Before class, find several relevant images and perform a reverse image search with each one to make sure you retrieve results that will be useful.
- Prior to leading the discussion, consider the responses you hope to elicit from the prompts, such as finding better image sources; tracking down an original image; locating higher quality, or larger, versions of an image; finding citation information; and identifying instances of plagiarism.

OPTIONAL EXTENSIONS

- Try this activity with TinEye Reverse Image Search (https://www.tineye .com) and compare results.
- Use the Google Image Quiz (http://google-image-quiz.net) as a warm-up. This dynamic game, created by Italian artist and researcher Silvio Lorusso, is a twist on the reverse search concept. You see an image and guess the Google query that retrieved it.

VISUAL LITERACY STANDARDS CONNECTION

- ACRL Visual Literacy Standard 2, Performance Indicators 1 and 2

Reverse Image Searching

Find an image related to your research topic, then perform a reverse image search and explore the results.

What options are there for narrowing and filtering the results?

_____

_____

_____

_____

Look at the image measurements. What is the range of sizes available for this image?

_____

_____

Can you find images that are visually similar? What do you notice about the similar images?

_____

_____

_____

_____

What is one website that includes your image?

_____

List one new idea _or_ one question that this reverse image search raised:

_____

_____

_____

Create and Use Images

IMAGES CAN ENLIVEN projects of all types by adding dimension and immediacy to everyday and academic communications. Digital technologies make this visual communication easier than ever. *Meaningful* visual communication, however, can be a challenge. Too often, images are an afterthought in a project and end up detracting from, rather than enhancing, the ideas and information being presented. Images can even work against the goals of a project, complicating rather than clarifying meanings.

In this chapter we share several approaches you can use to ensure that your visual communications are effective and meaningful. Align your visuals and project goals by knowing how images function to convey information and by using a rhetorical approach to image use. Achieve visual impact through an awareness of visual design principles and just the right amount of technical knowledge. Practice editing and creating visual materials to build your confidence and competence.

Foundational Questions

What Role Will Images Play in My Project?

Before you incorporate an image, spend some time thinking about the role that visuals will play. What ideas or information

ACTIVITIES IN THIS CHAPTER

are you trying to communicate? Are you creating images to convey a concept or to make an argument? Will your visuals serve to illustrate a process or point, or will they be decorative? Are you representing data graphically to tell a story? Now imagine your audience and align the visual content with the purpose of your project. Your answers to these questions will help you determine whether you will need to create a new image or use an existing one.

What Design Strategies Will I Use?

Creating useful visuals and using images effectively involve design strategies and a healthy dose of creativity. Think about the visual style of your project—is it serious, jaunty, moving, funny, or factual? What emotions do you want to evoke in your audience, if any? What do you want your audience to learn or consider by way of the images you're using? Thinking through these issues helps you to make intentional and meaningful aesthetic choices to communicate your message.

What Tools and Technologies Will Be Helpful?

Whether you are creating an image yourself or incorporating existing visual materials into your work, there are many tools and technologies to help you through the process. Experimenting with these image-production tools, and developing a level of proficiency with them, will help you create and adapt images to suit your purposes.

Are My Visuals Good? Could They Be Better?

Taking a step back to evaluate the visual products you create and the effect of the images you use is an essential part of the visual communication process. You'll want to assess your visuals to determine whether they meet your project goals. If the project is scholarly, you'll want to be sure that the visuals follow your discipline's conventions. After all, visual materials contribute to research, learning, and communication in most fields. Before revising your work, you can apply strategies for checking in with others to assess the effectiveness of your visual products.

The Power of Images

We've all heard the adage "A picture is worth a thousand words." Though not literally true, the saying captures the fact that imagery conveys meaning and information differently than language. It turns out that images are uniquely powerful because of the way the human brain processes visual information.

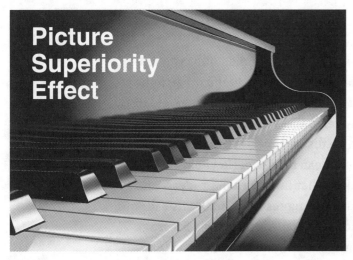

Figure 3.1.
Picture superiority effect

Memory experiments by cognitive psychologist Allan Paivio demonstrated that pictures are remembered better than words, a finding called the *picture superiority effect*. Paivio concluded that pictures access meaning more fully than words and are processed more deeply in the brain.

When you look at an image of a piano, for example, your brain is processing the information (perceiving, understanding, and remembering) by accessing two systems or channels—verbal and visual. You recognize the image and call up the words *piano* and *ivory* and *keys*. However, if you read or hear the word *piano,* you access only the verbal system. Of course, you can create a mental image of a piano without an accompanying picture, but the picture superiority effect still means that you will remember the word and meaning better if an image is conjured in your mind's eye, and providing an image helps the brain do that work.

This is not to say that we should ditch all text from our PowerPoint slides and library guides. Psychologist Richard Mayer's (2009) research on multimedia learning found that the visual and verbal channels complement each other. When pictures and words are integrated, as in figure 3.1, learners are able to construct a deeper understanding than if presented with words or pictures alone. The main takeaway is to think about how you can use visuals to amplify your messages across a wide range of contexts—whether it's a poster, a handout, or a classroom lesson.

Figure 3.2.
A typical slide combining text and image

Consider figure 3.2, which depicts a typical slide layout with text in bullet points accompanied by a small image. This slide essentially negates the picture superiority effect. Like figure 3.1, it contains a combination of image and text, but there is so much text that it overwhelms the viewer's perception of the image and encourages reading rather than listening or looking. No matter what a presenter might be saying when the slide is shown, if you're in the audience, you're probably just reading the words, and you're reading them faster than any presenter could ever deliver the content. You're likely not fully listening to what is being said or even really seeing the picture.

In *Presentation Zen,* communication expert Garr Reynolds dubs the tendency to include too much information on a slide *slideumentation,* a term he coined by combining *slide* with *documentation.* Reynolds urges presenters to avoid conflating visual aids with lengthy textual descriptions; he suggests that speakers think of presentations in three distinct pieces: visuals, speaker notes, and handouts for material the audience can read later (Reynolds 2008). Next time you create a visual product, ask: "What information or ideas am I representing with the written word that I could represent visually instead?" The answer just might surprise you. Use **Activity 3.2: Amplifying a Message with Visuals** to practice presenting information with images instead of text.

Aligning Image Use and Purpose

There are many ways to communicate with images: from providing illustration and decoration to presenting complex data with charts, graphs, and other visualizations. Images can be used as symbols to represent concepts or to provide visual cues or prompts that influence behavior or call for action.

When you are planning for image use, your purpose and context inform your message and design choices. Analyze the rhetorical situation to ensure that your image use aligns with your overall project goals. The Aristotelian concepts of *ethos, pathos,* and *logos* comprise the rhetorical triangle (figure 3.3), and taking the time to think through these concepts will guide your visual communication.

- Ethos—Depiction of character
    Ask: How am I portraying myself as the *author* or *creator*?
- Pathos—Emotional style or treatment
    Ask: Does my creation appeal to my *audience*?
- Logos—Discourse and reason
    Ask: Are the structure and content of my *message* strong?

The rhetorical triangle aligns your content with your project goals and context. You might be surprised by how much a few simple questions can clar-

Figure 3.3. *The rhetorical triangle*

Figure 3.4.
Ducks in a row

ify and improve your message. Let's think through an example.

Imagine that Molly A. Librarian is planning a workshop for a group of new faculty about citation management tools. She wants to express the benefits of these tools in a fun and engaging way, and the first thing that comes to mind is "getting your ducks in a row," so she searches for an image of ducks and finds a high-quality image of a line of rubber duckies called "Concept of Organization with Ducks in a Row." She uses the image as the opening slide for her presentation (figure 3.4).

Perfect, right?

Not so fast. Working this way helps capture ideas, but it's worth the extra step of thinking through what the image is communicating. Let's run through the questions for ethos, pathos, and logos for this scenario.

- *Ethos*—How is the author or creator portraying herself?
  Although Molly intends this image as lighthearted and fun, it may not help her to present herself as a serious professional, potentially undermining her credibility with her audience. She could unintentionally be presenting herself as uninformed about the nature of faculty work, potentially alienating those whom she is trying to reach.

- *Pathos*—Does the creation appeal to the audience?
  Although this image is appealing as a visual of rubber ducks, it may not make sense to the new faculty members who are attending Molly's workshop to learn to use a citation management tool. There is a risk that they will find the image juvenile and disconnected from their experience as accomplished researchers. There is also the possibility that they may not be familiar with the phrase "ducks in a row," so the underlying idiom and its meaning would be lost.

- *Logos*—Are the structure and content of the message strong?
  Molly's overall workshop goal is to communicate the importance of organizing research to new professors at her institution. This image choice does not align with that message. It also relies on a narrow and culturally specific use of language and could unintentionally alienate learners with diverse life experiences.

What can Molly A. Librarian do? She can reexamine her purpose and context and come up with a better idea. Molly wants to portray herself as a serious librarian with a sense of humor who knows a thing or two about citation management. She plans to appeal to the emotion of the new faculty by convincing them that there is a better way to organize their research process. She hopes to communicate clearly and effectively with every individual attending the workshop. Perhaps a desk covered in documents waiting to be filed will grab the audience's attention and include all learners, while still letting Molly's personality shine through. Searching for "messy desk" uncovers gems such as figure 3.5 that will better suit this workshop.

Figure 3.5.
Pile of documents

The preceding example illustrates the importance of keeping your specific circumstances in mind when using images and being flexible enough to pivot when your first image choice fails to meet your goals. Idioms, wordplay, homonyms, and colloquialisms do not always translate well into visual representations, and they need to be used with caution. At their worst, attempts at clever image use can create confusion and detract from the learning experience. Learners bring diverse life circumstances and experiences to the classroom, and you can use ethos, pathos, and logos to ensure that your images are inclusive. Knowing your audience also alerts you to situations in which you need textual equivalents and different types of images to reach all learners. Student work is often rooted in a disciplinary context, and **Activity 3.1: Exploring Disciplinary Image Use** identifies ways that images are used within a discipline and applies this knowledge to inform an upcoming project.

Designing and Making Images

If asked to come up with a synonym for *design,* you might say *creativity.* Indeed, design requires creativity, but they are not the same thing. The good news is that creativity can be learned. David Kelley, founder of IDEO, a leader in the user-centered design of products, services, and environments, wrote *Creative Confidence* with his brother, Tom. The Kelley brothers' premise is that "creativity is something you practice, not just a talent you're born with" (Kelley and Kelley 2013). The International Center for Studies in Creativity at Buffalo State University supports this view of creativity and defines it as "the production of original ideas that serve a purpose."

DESIGN BASICS

You can exercise your creativity by learning about and employing the basic design strategies covered in this section, including color, texture, shape, typography, contrast, repetition, alignment, and composition. These design concepts help you and your students to think about the formal elements of images and how they impact the delivery, interpretation, and meaning of visual information. There are also many great resources to help build your confidence in this area—see our list of **Favorite Books on Design and Visual Communication** for suggestions.

Color

Color is the combination of *hue* (e.g., red, yellow, and blue), *intensity* (brightness or dullness), and *value* (lightness or darkness). The color wheel, comprising twelve colors, helps designers choose color schemes that work together. The points of the triangles in the center of figure 3.6 show two triads: yellow/blue/red and green/violet/orange.

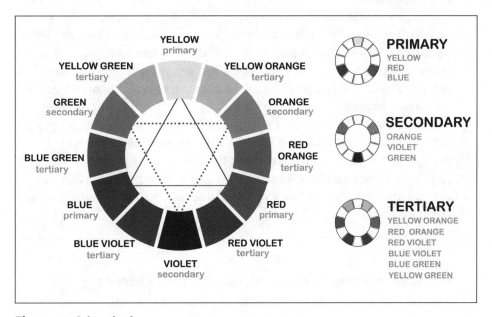

Figure 3.6. *Color wheel*

Basic Principles

- There are three *primary* colors: yellow, red, and blue.
- *Secondary* colors combine two primary colors: they are orange, violet, and green.
- *Tertiary* colors combine a primary and a secondary color: they are yellow orange, red orange, red violet, blue violet, blue green, and yellow green.

Colors and Culture

Aesthetic elements such as color, line, shape, and texture play a significant role in the suggestive or associative meanings that a viewer perceives from an image. Color may suggest feelings, such as anger or happiness, or ideas, such as power or strength.

Color has different meanings and evokes different feelings and emotions across cultures. A study conducted by Dr. Ralph B. Hupka, a specialist in the psychology of emotion at California State University, Long Beach, and a cross-cultural team of researchers gives us a glimpse into varied associations with color (Hupka et al. 1997). The team looked at the emotional impact of color across five countries—the United States, Germany, Mexico, Poland, and Russia. The researchers looked at color associations with four emotions: anger, envy, fear, and jealousy. The results suggest that the emotions associated with color have a strong cultural component. Although all countries in the sample associated black with anger and fear, and red with anger and jealousy, there was great variation with associations of purple, green, and yellow.

Other researchers' work also supports the finding that color associations vary across cultures. Writing from a marketing and communication perspective, Mubeen Aslam points out that white is often associated with purity in Western cultures but with death and mourning in some Eastern cultures (Aslam 2006). Arianne Jennifer Rourke and Zena O'Connor, design researchers from the Universities of Sydney and New South Wales, observe that color associations vary not only across cultures but also within the contexts in which they are used. The color red, for example, is often used in conjunction with revolutionary ideas. Communism and socialism have often been represented by a red star. Red is also used to represent dangerous situations, as indicated by stop signs and danger signs (Rourke and O'Connor 2012).

- *Complementary* colors are directly opposite each other on the color wheel and provide high contrast (e.g., yellow and violet).
- *Analogous* colors are groups of three adjacent colors on the color wheel (e.g., yellow green, green, and blue green).
- A *triad* is composed of any three colors that form a triangle on the color wheel (e.g., green, orange, and violet). Using a triad to compose a palette can create well-balanced, bold combinations.
- A *monochromatic* palette consists of one color varied in intensity from light to dark.

COFFEE BREAK!

Experiment with Color

What are your institution's colors?

Use these colors as a starting point to create a complementary, analogous, triad, and monochromatic palette.

Use *Color Picker* and *Color Mixer* from W3Schools to try out different colors and color combinations. These tools also will give you the hex codes to use the colors in Web environments.

Texture

Texture is the perceived surface quality of a design. Together, the rough and smooth rocks in figure 3.7 provide contrast and visual interest.

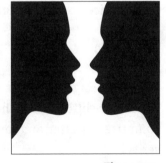

Figure 3.7.
Smooth and rough textures

Basic Principles

- Texture may be rough, smooth, soft, shiny, or some other quality.
- Texture can create a distinctive feeling within a design.
- Texture can be used to create and maintain interest.

Put It into Practice

- Use a texture as a background for a presentation. How does the texture change the feel?
- Enhance a photograph by changing the texture. What impact does this change have?

Shape

Shape is the area that is outlined within a design. The well-known figure-ground illusion known as the "Rubin vase" or "Rubin face-vase," shown in figure 3.8, plays with shape and helps to explain the concept of negative space.

Figure 3.8.
Positive and negative space

Basic Principles

- Shapes can be geometric or organic.
- Shapes can be *positive* or *negative* depending on how they are used. Positive shapes are in the foreground, while negative shapes are in the background.
- Silhouettes are useful for understanding where positive and negative spaces lie.

Favorite Books on Design and Visual Communication

Beautiful Evidence by Edward R. Tufte (2006)

Design Principles by Richard Poulin (2011)

Graphic Design: The New Basics by Ellen Lupton and Jennifer Cole Phillips (2015)

The Language of Graphic Design by Richard Poulin (2011)

The Non-Designer's Design Book by Robin Williams (2008)

Presentation Zen by Garr Reynolds (2008)

slide:ology by Nancy Duarte (2008)

Thinking with Type by Ellen Lupton (2010)

- The lines that distinguish shapes serve to set them off from the rest of the design.
- Shapes can be differentiated through color, texture, or use of light and dark.
- Shapes may be used in different combinations to direct the viewer's focus.

Put It into Practice

- Look at a book jacket or a poster and identify the positive and negative spaces.
- Use shape as a signature design element. A solid shape rendered in different sizes or colors can provide a unifying yet attention-grabbing visual theme.
- Trace the outlines of shapes in an advertisement, then step back and notice how the design uses shapes and space.

Figure 3.9.
Serif and sans serif fonts

Typography

Typography is the arrangement and style of lettering within a design. The text in figure 3.9 shows serif fonts, which have little lines at the ends of the strokes (*serifs*) that comprise the letter, and sans serif fonts, which do not have serifs.

Basic Principles

- The choice of type should generally maximize readability in terms of size, spacing, and contrast. Remember that fonts must, first and foremost, be readable.

The Quick Brown Fox Jumps Over The Lazy Dog.
ABCDEFGHIJKLMNOPQRSTUVWXYZ
abcdefghijklmnopqrstuvwxyz 0123456789

The Quick Brown Fox Jumps Over The Lazy Dog.
abcdefghijklmnopqrstuvwxyz0123456789

- Fonts may be *serif* (having small lines attached to the ends of letters) or *sans serif* (without these lines).
- There are no hard-and-fast rules for when to use serif or sans serif fonts, but some designers suggest using serif for text in print and sans serif for large, multimedia text. Most e-readers seem to adhere to this maxim, and Amazon's Bookerly font is a good example.
- Fonts can be combined for impact and visual interest, but be aware that using three or more different fonts within a single design can be distracting, as can the use of overly fancy or cartoonish fonts.
- Typography has a long and rich history, and font choice is an important part of a design strategy. It affects the overall style and meaning of your visual presentation.

Put It into Practice

- Does your institution use a specific font? If you're not sure, check with your institution's office of communications. Is it serif or sans serif? Are there guidelines for this font's usage? Can you find a font that complements it?
- Experiment with writing the same message in different fonts. Your message may take on different meanings or evoke particular styles or periods depending on the font you use.

Figure 3.10.
Contrast

Contrast

Contrast is the juxtaposition of different elements within a design. Contrast adds visual interest and creates emphasis. The color, shape, and texture of the half apple in figure 3.10 contrast with those of the other apples.

Basic Principles

- Contrast may be created using many different elements, such as color, type, texture, line thickness, and shape.
- Contrast can be used to highlight elements in an image, to create interest, and to show the viewer what is most important.
- When used with type, contrast emphasizes words or phrases.

Put It into Practice

- Look at an advertisement. How is contrast used to emphasize the message?
- Open a slide that contains two different objects, images, or pieces of text. Experiment with various ways to make these items as different as possible. Make bold choices.

Repetition

Repetition is the use of similar elements within a design. In figure 3.11, the repeated cup shape creates consistency and unity within the design while allowing the viewer to quickly discern the differences among the thirty-two types of coffee drinks.

Basic Principles

- Repetition creates unity within an image and helps to make information easier for the viewer to interpret.
- Repetition makes it easy for the viewer to quickly discern the differences among different types.
- Elements such as colors, shapes, lines, fonts, and objects can be repeated throughout a design.
- Too much variation can be distracting and can make it difficult to guide the focus of the viewer.

Figure 3.11.
Repetition of coffee types

Alignment

Alignment is the placement of elements so as to create lines within a design. The text and images in figure 3.12 are center-aligned along three invisible vertical lines and three invisible horizontal lines. The alignment creates strong organization within the piece, showing the unity that exists among the nine different innovation activities. Alignment makes the image more visually appealing and makes the information easier to interpret.

Basic Principles

- Alignment helps to clarify the organization of elements within a design.
- Consistent alignment creates organization among different elements.
- Lines may be visible or invisible. Even when there are no visible lines in an image, the placement of items

Figure 3.12.
Alignment among innovation activities

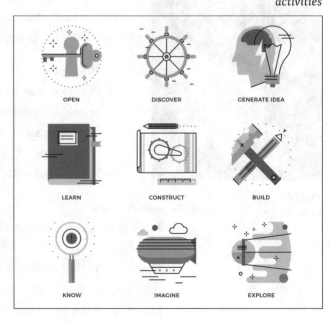

COFFEE BREAK!

Practice Repetition and Alignment

Pull up an old slide presentation (or use a Creative Commons–licensed presentation).

REPETITION

Identify the elements that are repeated. Consider headings, bullet points, icons, colors, and images. How do these elements affect how you view the presentation?

Now try repeating an element such as an image, shape, or text feature throughout the entire presentation. What effect does this repetition create?

ALIGNMENT

Experiment with moving everything to the left, right, and center. What happens?

Now line everything up on one or two strong lines. How do these changes affect how you view the slide?

in relation to each other creates alignment, making the information easier to interpret.

Put It into Practice

- Explore a restaurant menu. Pull a takeout menu from your desk drawer, or find an image of one online. Examine the alignment. Is text aligned to the left, to the right, or in the center? Or are several alignments in use? How does alignment affect the menu's readability?

Composition

Composition is the arrangement of elements within a design. The "rule of thirds" is a composition technique that uses two horizontal and two vertical lines to divide an image and inform the layout. Figure 3.13 illustrates this rule: The fisherman's head and waist are located at two of the intersections, with his body following one of the lines. The horizon follows another line, and the trees on the horizon are close to a third intersection. Even though the subject of the image is off center, the photograph appears balanced and feels natural.

Figure 3.13. *Rule of thirds*

Basic Principles

- A grid based on the rule of thirds helps to achieve balance and emphasis in a composition.
- Grouping items together helps to organize content, making it easier to interpret.
- Placing objects close together can suggest that they are related, while placing objects far apart may suggest that they are different.
- White space, or negative space, is an important part of overall composition: don't be afraid of it!

Put It into Practice

- Take several photos of the same subject and use the rule of thirds to practice putting your subject in different parts of the image. What happens when you place your subject in the center? What happens when you use the rule of thirds and place your subject along one of the lines or at an intersection of the lines?
- Put a piece of tracing paper over an advertisement and draw an evenly spaced grid over the ad. Now trace the figures in the advertisement. What do you notice about the use of white space? Do you see the rule of thirds at work?
- Use the rule of thirds to inform your design by imagining grid lines (or drawing them in) the next time you create a handout or slide presentation.

Design Tips for Visualizing Data

In chapter 1, "Interpret and Analyze Images," we discussed the characteristics of graphics and questions to consider when reading them. On the flipside is the ability to know how to visually represent the data you have. Here we present a few best practices to keep in mind once you have chosen a format to visualize your data. Consult **More to Explore: Visualizing Data** in chapter 1 to dive deeper. In **Activity 3.4: Creating Graphical Representations of Data,** students will practice grappling with these design choices.

EXPLORE AND CHOOSE FORMAT

The nature of your data and your communication goal should guide your choice of format or chart type. For example, time series data are well presented as a line chart. It is also useful to explore variations because some visualizations emphasize certain aspects of the data in different ways. Once you have chosen a format, you will encounter a new series of design choices and considerations.

ARRANGE ELEMENTS DELIBERATELY

Be purposeful about positioning and emphasizing elements to focus your viewer's attention on the most important aspects of the data. The nature of the data should guide a logical organization (e.g., by time period, alphabetically, by frequency, etc.) and layout (e.g., proportion, scale, aspect ratio, etc.) for a readable and statistically accurate display. For instance, a bar chart can be arranged from highest to lowest, which gives viewers a quick comparative summary, rather than arranged randomly, which is visually unhelpful. Close placement of text with its associated data speeds up comprehension: whenever possible place labels near the data instead of in a legend; if a legend is necessary, put it near the data it represents.

PROVIDE EXPLANATION WITH TEXT

Give your audience the necessary information, and don't assume viewers know what everything in the graphic means. Make sure you label the data, axes, and units concisely, and include proper citation for external data sources. Use fonts that are simple and legible. The typography should support, not distract from, the data.

USE COLOR WISELY

Color is used for differentiating labels, distinguishing values, and creating an engaging and effective visualization. Color should be applied intentionally to communicate your message and to improve the readability of the graphic. Use the following guidelines.

Continued on page 80

Design Tips for Visualizing Data (continued)

- *Choose a color scheme:* Select an appropriate color palette and use it consistently. ColorBrewer 2.0 is a color picker designed for mapping, but it also works for other visualizations.
- *Make colors accessible:* Keep color-blind viewers (5 to 10 percent of the population) in mind and avoid color combinations such as red/green and blue/yellow. Simulator programs are available to check for color blindness. Color should not be the sole way to differentiate items.
- *Highlight and order data:* A change of color or contrast signifies a change or addition in the data. For presentation purposes, use one or two colors for emphasizing data and patterns, and use color-coding for organization and hierarchy.
- *Consider meaning:* Does your color scheme create a feeling or meaning that relates to your data, or does it confuse your viewer? A gray scale can effectively differentiate categories, whereas colors often generate what Edward Tufte (2001) terms "graphical puzzles" because the rainbow spectrum doesn't readily or naturally render a meaningful visual order. For some types of data though, physically and culturally resonant colors may aid readability, such as green for apples and blue for blueberries in a graphic depicting fruit sales (Lin et al. 2013). The bottom line is that color should add visual clarity.

TELL THE TRUTH WITH YOUR DATA

Some charts bring with them certain pitfalls to watch out for. When creating charts, keep the following guidelines in mind.

- *Apply the "start at zero rule":* In bar charts the y-axis must start at zero, otherwise the visual difference between values can be overemphasized. Breaking this rule can make a minor change look more meaningful than it really is. Although line charts don't need to start at zero, take care to choose an appropriate y-axis scale and increments so as not to exaggerate or minimize the trend.
- *Consider the suitable aspect ratio:* In some charts, such as line charts, the same data can look different depending on the aspect ratio of the chart. But how do you know what aspect ratio is appropriate for your data? In photographs you can see clearly whether the aspect ratio is being stretched or squished, but in charts and graphs such distortion is less obvious. One best practice—though not a hard-and-fast rule—is for the average slope in a line chart to be 45 degrees, known as "banking to 45 degrees" (Cleveland, McGill, and McGill 1988). This practice creates a chart that is "standard" and easier to interpret clearly.

TECHNOLOGY AND IMAGES

When creating and using images, knowing about design principles is just one piece of the puzzle. You also need to be able to put the design principles into practice. Fortunately, many tools and technologies are available for creating and adapting images. Tools and best practices are constantly changing, so make experimentation and a regular reading of technology reviews and blogs standard parts of your professional development practices.

The key to choosing and using technology effectively is to articulate what you need to *do* with it. In this section, we lay out some core vocabulary related to editing and formatting images. These terms are common to image-manipulation tools from Photoshop to Paint, web-based tools, and even your mobile phone. When you're comfortable with image manipulation vocabulary, you'll easily find the right tool for the job by conducting a simple web search or by exploring the tools in standard software packages. Try **Activity 3.5: Editing Images** to give students an opportunity to experiment with image editing and to discuss changes that image manipulation can make to appearance, design, and meaning. Use the **Image Editing Basics** chart and corresponding **Coffee Break!** to practice editing techniques.

Image Editing Basics

TERM	DEFINITION
Blur	Soften the focus of the image so that it appears indistinct or fuzzy
Contrast	Difference between the amount of light and dark in an image
Crop	Cut out portions of an image
Filter	Overlay or effect applied to an image that changes its color or style
Outlines and borders	Lines drawn around items within an image or around a whole image
Recolor	Change colors within an image or adjust the degree of color saturation
Reformat	Convert an image to a different file format (e.g., jpeg, png)
Resize	Make an image smaller or larger
Rotate	Change the orientation or alignment of an image
Shadow	Effect that gives the appearance of depth or three-dimensionality
Transparency	Adjustment of part or all of an image so that light passes through

A digital image is an encoded data file. The image formatting specifications are contained within the data, including a description of the properties of the image, such as the size and resolution. When you are working with a digital image, it helps to understand basic formatting terminology to describe image specifications, such as those shown in the **Image Formatting Basics** chart.

Image Formatting Basics

TERM	DEFINITION
Aspect ratio	The ratio of width to height of an image expressed as width:height—for example, 4:3 (traditional); 16:9 (widescreen).
Color codes	There are two models for communicating colors: RGB and CMYK. RGB, used in computing, combines red (R), green (G), and blue (B) light to produce a broad array of colors. The RGB level of each color is expressed as a value between 0 and 255 (e.g., pink is 255,192,203, which equates to a hex code of FFC0CB). The CMYK color system, used in the print industry, uses cyan (C), magenta (M), yellow (Y), and black (K) to produce different ink shades. Values are represented with percentages (e.g., pink is C = 0%, M = 24.71%, Y = 20.39%, and K = 0%).
Dimensions	The height and width of an image, measured in pixels, inches, or centimeters. Also referred to as "image size."
File format	The format in which data is stored; common image file formats include jpg, jpeg, gif, png, and tiff. Each of these formats has a specified organization of the data within the file. Different file formats are preferable for different situations. For instance, jpeg is considered "lossy," meaning its integrity can be compromised through use and over time, whereas tiff is an archival and preservation format.
File size	The size of a digital image file, usually measured in kilobytes (KB) or megabytes (MB).
Resolution	The density or amount of detail in a digital image, often measured in ppi (pixels per inch). Higher resolution images include more detail and are sharper.

You will need different image sizes, formats, and resolutions, depending on how and where you will be using your image. Our **Image Formats and Resolutions for Common Uses** chart provides some general guidelines for aligning image specifications with common tasks and image uses. Keep the following technical best practices in mind when editing image specifications:

COFFEE BREAK!

Edit an Image

Choose an image and open the editing tool of your choice. Experiment with as many of the following edits as you can.

Blur	Outlines and borders	Rotate
Contrast	Recolor	Shadow
Crop	Reformat	Transparency
Filter	Resize	

Which edits might you apply in your own work?

- *Create or download the highest quality image file.* Images can always be made smaller or compressed. If you anticipate that you will need a large image (for print or detailed display, archival preservation, etc.), download or create the largest possible image file, then resize it as needed.
- *Retain a master.* Keep an unedited original version of your image so you can start over if you make a mistake during the editing process.
- *Resize first.* Resize your image in an image editing tool before inserting the image into presentation software or uploading it to a website, blog, and the like. If you insert an image into a software tool or online environment before resizing, the result might be an unexpected display size or overly large file size, which could impact download speed.
- *Don't "upsize."* Consider the image's original size and resolution to be the maximum. Do not "upsize," or make larger, a new digital image from a smaller digital image. This will result in a blurry or pixelated image.
- *Be mindful of "downsizing."* Making a smaller image from a large image and then saving it loses the larger dimensions and resolution of the original image, and you will lose quality if you make the image larger again.
- *Maintain the aspect ratio.* Always retain the original aspect ratio when resizing images. Changing the aspect ratio will distort the image. Crop, rather than resize, if you need to edit an image to specific dimensions.

Image Formats and Resolutions for Common Uses

Note that dimensions and resolutions are approximate and should be considered starting points.

USE OR ENVIRONMENT	FILE FORMAT	DIMENSIONS (SIZE, IN PIXELS) AND RESOLUTION (PPI)	EXPLANATIONS AND RECOMMENDATIONS
Presentation	jpeg	*Dimensions:* 1024x768 or 1280x960 (full-screen, 4:3 ratio, XGA projector) 1920x1080 (full-screen, 16:9 ratio, HD projector) *Resolution:* 72 or 96 ppi	Projector capabilities determine optimal image presentation size. XGA projectors are most common in academic and conference venues and project 4:3 ratio images. If you are using full-screen images, plan to use 4:3 ratio images to avoid image distortion, unless you are able to confirm 16:9 HD projection is available. Smaller images can be any size or ratio.
Blog post	jpeg	*Dimensions:* 160x120 (thumbnail) 300x225 (small) 660x495 (medium) 1024x768 (large) 1280x960 (full) *Resolution:* 72 or 96 ppi	Choose image dimensions for blog posts based on your purpose and desired effect. Experiment to determine which sizes work best for you. Screen display resolution is typically maximized at 72 ppi, although 96 ppi is becoming more common. Resolutions higher than 96 ppi do not provide greater on-screen clarity.
Website	jpeg	*Dimensions:* 1024x768 to 1280x960 (full-screen background image) *Resolution:* 72 or 96 ppi	Computer screen resolutions vary considerably. W3Schools reports that 97 percent of their site visitors have a screen resolution 1024÷768 pixels or higher. If you want to display a full-screen image without scrolling for most users, aim for 1024÷768.
Online research guide	jpeg	*Dimensions:* 300x225 (small) 660x495 (medium) *Resolution:* 72 or 96 ppi	Small or medium-sized images are recommended for research guides because they are easily visible but do not occupy an inordinate amount of screen space.
Print poster	jpeg	*Dimensions:* Varied, depending on your design and project purpose. *Resolution:* 300 dpi will produce the sharpest print images	Make sure your images are large enough to be easily visible. Generally, images should not be smaller than 300÷225 on print posters.
Screenshot	jpeg, png, or gif	*Dimensions:* Varied, depending on the screen area you capture *Resolution:* Will be the same as the native resolution of your screen, so 72 or 96 ppi	Choose jpeg for the smallest screenshot file size. The png format renders text, color, and web graphics more clearly than jpeg, but yields a larger file size. Use gif for animations.
Master archival scan of print materials	tiff	*Dimensions:* Varied, depending on the size of the print original *Resolution:* Scan to 600 ppi	Consult your library's guidelines for archival and preservation scanning. Different formats (35 mm slides, print photographs, newspapers) require different settings.

☕ COFFEE BREAK!

Explore Image Formatting

Choose an image, and find out as many of these formatting details as you can.

Dimensions: _____

Resolution (in ppi): _____

File format: _____

File size: _____

How might you apply this information in your work?

_____

_____

PRACTICE MAKING

A key part of Kelley and Kelley's definition of creativity is "practice" (2013). Pradeep Sharma, former dean of Architecture + Design at the Rhode Island School of Design and now provost, says that design *is* a practice, which "implies two things: first, that we have to do something in order to understand it; and second, that we get better the more we do it" (Somerson and Hermano 2013). Understanding how design works requires doing it. The more you practice design and make visual products, the more you will experience how design communicates through visual forms, creates meaning, and tells stories. And, of course, your visual communications will become sharper.

Getting started with a *practice* of making visuals can feel like a hurdle, even to seasoned artists and designers. Clara Lieu, visual artist, notes in her "Ask the Art Professor" column in the Huffington Post in 2014 that grand ideas and ambitions for significant projects can create a barrier to doing anything at all. She suggests, "Instead of embarking on some huge project, start a series of daily exercises for at least one month." This strategy of small daily practice can work well for anyone wanting to venture into making of any kind. Try using one of this chapter's "Put It into Practice" features or "Coffee Breaks" each day for a week to build your experience and comfort with making. Storyboarding is another way of thinking through a visual project by breaking it down into smaller parts. Use **Activity 3.3: Storyboarding** to practice this technique with students.

The process of making can also be the goal of the activity. Critical making is an approach to solving problems that uses the physical act of manipulating tactile materials or technology in order to work through questions or interrogate sites of confusion or conflict. Matt Ratto, associate professor in the Faculty of Information at the University of Toronto, coined the term *critical making* in 2008 as a convergence of critical thinking and making practices. He defines critical making as "a series of processes that attempt to connect humanistic practices of conceptual and scholarly exploration to design methodologies including storyboarding, brainstorming and bodystorming, and prototyping" (Abel et al. 2011). Making something visual can be an effective way to think through a complex topic or vexing problem and can lead to a critical-visual approach to a research question.

As libraries increasingly engage with making activities, some are developing makerspaces complete with tools, software, and participatory learning opportunities. Visual literacy activities and concepts, such as producing visual materials for a range of projects and using design strategies and creativity in image and visual media production, can be realized in library spaces. Makerspaces in libraries combine outreach and fun with the critical work of design and making. These activities support library learning goals, enrich library instructional programs, and provide grounding for bringing visual literacy learning outcomes into this worthwhile area of exploration and practice.

Evaluating Visual Products

Just as you would never hand in the first draft of a paper, it is important to review, reflect upon, critique, and revise the visual materials you create. You can employ techniques from design fields to help students and colleagues critique work, in addition to more familiar strategies such as peer review and checklists.

Use these reflection questions to assess the effectiveness of your visuals:

- Do other people understand what I am trying to communicate? How do I know?
- What might be ambiguous or confusing about my visuals?
- How can I improve or clarify my visuals?
- Are my design choices helping or hindering my overall visual communication?
- Is my visual product consistent with conventions in my field?

- Does my visual product meet my project goals?
- What will I do next?

Use **Activity 3.6: Design Critique** to guide students, and colleagues, through the process of critiquing visual products.

There may be occasions when you, or your faculty, need to formally evaluate student visual products or students' use of images in projects. Ideally, you'll want to consider how effectively the student's visual choices communicate her research or creative ideas *and* how well she deploys design strategies. When evaluating student work, rubrics that focus on the criteria in the assignment can help. Adapt our **Evaluating Visual Products Handout** (see page 88) to suit your needs.

Evaluating Visual Products

Use some or all of these scales to evaluate a visual product.

Meaning Image use, or visual presentation, supports the project thesis, question, or intended meaning.

☐ *Strongly Disagree*   ☐ *Disagree*   ☐ *Neutral*   ☐ *Agree*   ☐ *Strongly Agree*

Style Visual style is appropriate to the project and intended audience.

☐ *Strongly Disagree*   ☐ *Disagree*   ☐ *Neutral*   ☐ *Agree*   ☐ *Strongly Agree*

Technology and Medium Technologies used and chosen media complement and enhance project goals and meaning.

☐ *Strongly Disagree*   ☐ *Disagree*   ☐ *Neutral*   ☐ *Agree*   ☐ *Strongly Agree*

Scholarly Use and Citation Images are used as scholarly products and are cited, credited, or captioned as appropriate.

☐ *Strongly Disagree*   ☐ *Disagree*   ☐ *Neutral*   ☐ *Agree*   ☐ *Strongly Agree*

Clarity Content is easy to read with appropriate use of fonts, background, and formatting.

☐ *Strongly Disagree*   ☐ *Disagree*   ☐ *Neutral*   ☐ *Agree*   ☐ *Strongly Agree*

Cohesiveness All elements are coordinated with the visual design.

☐ *Strongly Disagree*   ☐ *Disagree*   ☐ *Neutral*   ☐ *Agree*   ☐ *Strongly Agree*

Layout Layout uses horizontal and vertical white space appropriately.

☐ *Strongly Disagree*   ☐ *Disagree*   ☐ *Neutral*   ☐ *Agree*   ☐ *Strongly Agree*

Balance Images and text are well placed in relation to each other and are used with proportion and balance.

☐ *Strongly Disagree*   ☐ *Disagree*   ☐ *Neutral*   ☐ *Agree*   ☐ *Strongly Agree*

Graphics Images are thoughtfully chosen and enhance the content.

☐ *Strongly Disagree*   ☐ *Disagree*   ☐ *Neutral*   ☐ *Agree*   ☐ *Strongly Agree*

Overall Design Overall visual design (including use of color, typography, and layout) is visually appealing and meets project goals.

☐ *Strongly Disagree*   ☐ *Disagree*   ☐ *Neutral*   ☐ *Agree*   ☐ *Strongly Agree*

Comments:

Next Steps

Design strategies help you think about and create visual communications. To continue building your confidence in image use and creation, try the following:

- Plan and storyboard your next outreach or teaching occasion.
- Apply basic design principles to a poster or presentation.
- Practice image editing and formatting.
- Use the design principles to evaluate a visual communication on your campus.

REFERENCES

Abel, Bas Van, Lucas Evers, Roel Klasseen, and Peter Troxler. 2011. *Open Design Now: Why Design Cannot Remain Exclusive*. Amsterdam, The Netherlands: BIS Publishers.

Aslam, Mubeen M. 2006. "Are You Selling the Right Colour? A Cross-Cultural Review of Colour as a Marketing Cue." *Journal of Marketing Communications* 12 (1): 15–30.

Cleveland, William S., Marylyn E. McGill, and Robert McGill. 1988. "The Shape Parameter of a Two-Variable Graph." *Journal of the American Statistical Association* 83 (402): 289–300.

Hupka, Ralph B., Zbigniew Zaleski, Jurgen Otto, Lucy Reidl, and Nadia V. Tarabrina. 1997. "The Colors of Anger, Envy, Fear, and Jealousy: A Cross-Cultural Study." *Journal of Cross-Cultural Psychology* 28 (2): 156–71.

Kelley, David, and Tom Kelley. 2013. *Creative Confidence: Unleashing the Creative Potential within Us All*. New York: Crown Publishing Group.

Lin, Sharon, Julie Fortuna, Chinmay Kulkarni, Maureen Stone, and Jeffrey Heer. 2013. "Selecting Semantically-Resonant Colors for Data Visualization." *Computer Graphics Forum (Proc. EuroVis)*. http://idl.cs.washington.edu/papers/semantically-resonant -colors.

Mayer, Richard E. 2009. *Multimedia Learning*. Cambridge: Cambridge University Press.

Reynolds, Garr. 2008. *Presentation Zen: Simple Ideas on Presentation Design and Delivery*. Berkeley, CA: New Riders.

Rourke, Arianne, and Zena O'Connor. 2012. *Effective Use of Visuals in Teaching in Higher Education*. Hauppauge, NY: Nova Science Publishers.

Somerson, Rosanne, and Mara Hermano. 2013. *The Art of Critical Making: Rhode Island School of Design on Creative Practice*. Hoboken, NJ: Wiley.

Tufte, Edward. 2001. *The Visual Display of Quantitative Information*. 2nd ed. Cheshire, CT: Graphics Press.

ACTIVITY 3.1

Exploring Disciplinary Image Use

LEARNING OUTCOMES
- Identify ways that images are used within a discipline.
- Plan for the use of images in an upcoming project.

DESCRIPTION

Students use library resources to find scholarly works related to a topic of interest or course research assignment. Next, students look at the types of images used by the authors and the type of information that each image is being used to convey. Students use the **Images and Disciplinary Communication Worksheet** to keep track of what they find. For example, if the subject is molecular biology, a student might find the following:

1. Ribbon diagram—used to represent protein structure
2. Mass spectrometry graph—used to represent the spatial distribution of a molecular sample
3. Sequence alignment—used to highlight sequences that are conserved across species

In engineering, a student might find the following:

1. Model—used to represent the structure of a building meant to withstand earthquakes
2. Photograph—used to show damage that occurred to a building as the result of an earthquake
3. Graph—used to show seismic test data

TIP FOR SUCCESS
- You may want to begin this activity by reviewing different types of images, such as tables, graphs, charts, diagrams, and so on. As students share the different types and uses of the images that they find, observe commonalities of image usage within a discipline or differences in image usage among different disciplines, as appropriate. This activity works well individually or in small groups.

VISUAL LITERACY STANDARDS CONNECTION
- ACRL Visual Literacy Standard 5, Performance Indicator 1

Images and Disciplinary Communication

Find three scholarly sources that are related to your topic and that contain *at least one* image, then complete the steps.

Step 1: List three to five different image types (e.g., table, chart, diagram, map, photograph, model, etc.) that you encounter, and describe each image's purpose.

SOURCE	IMAGE TYPE	IMAGE PURPOSE—WHAT DOES THE IMAGE CONVEY?
Example: Hattwig et al. (2012) article	*Example: array*	*Example: Depicts ACRL Visual Literacy Standards*

Step 2: Reflect on how you plan to use images.

Do your findings impact the types of images you might use in your research?

_____

_____

What information do you hope to convey with images?

_____

_____

Amplifying a Message with Visuals

LEARNING OUTCOMES

- Apply visual thinking skills to communicate a message.
- Experiment with increasing the visual impact of a message.

DESCRIPTION

Give students a text-heavy PowerPoint slide and ask them to circle all elements that could be represented visually. Instruct them to sketch a visual of a circled element. Students share their choices and their sketches. Then discuss how to apply this technique to amplify the impact of a message.

TIP FOR SUCCESS

- Make sure that the content of the PowerPoint slide is relevant to the students in the class.

OPTIONAL EXTENSIONS

- This activity is a good precursor to **Activity 3.3: Storyboarding.**
- As shown in the example, this activity can be adapted for a librarian professional development workshop.

VISUAL LITERACY STANDARDS CONNECTION

- ACRL Visual Literacy Standard 5, Performance Indicator 4
- ACRL Visual Literacy Standard 6, Performance Indicators 1 and 2

Amplifying a Message with Visuals

This example is from a workshop for librarians.

Checking Out Books

- How many books can you check out?
  - As many as you need
    (or can reasonably carry!)

- How long can you check out books?
  - For 28 days at a time
  - Renew through the Library Catalog
    » Remember to set up your PIN

  - late fees are 25 cents/day
    » Tip: Keep an eye on your account!

Step 1 Instructor asks participants to circle elements that can be represented visually.

Step 2 Each participant chooses one element to depict and sketches a visual.

Step 3 Participants share the elements they circled and their sketches.

Step 4 Instructor shares sample circled elements.

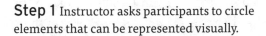
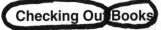
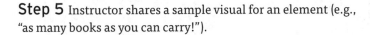

Checking Out Books

- How many books can you check out?
  - As many as you need
    (or can reasonably carry!)

- How long can you check out books?
  - For 28 days at a time
  - Renew through the Library Catalog
    » Remember to set up your PIN
  - late fees are 25 cents/day
    » Tip: Keep an eye on your account!

Step 5 Instructor shares a sample visual for an element (e.g., "as many books as you can carry!").

Step 6 Discuss how to apply this technique for creating messages.

Storyboarding

LEARNING OUTCOME
- Plan for the visual layout and design of a visual project.

DESCRIPTION

To prepare for a media project, students think about what they want their design to look like, then sketch it out in a storyboard. A storyboard provides the visual layout of content in a project and lists the basic elements that will be placed in each part of the design. Distribute a storyboard template, such as the one shown in the **Storyboard Template Worksheet**, to students. Ask students to roughly sketch their design in one or more boxes that represent each part of their media project. Text can be added below each drawing to list notes about the design or related image files.

TIP FOR SUCCESS
- Creating a storyboard does not require advanced artistic skill! It is best to keep the drawing simple and use stick figures or the like to represent design ideas. To get them started, show students an example or two, such as the following one.

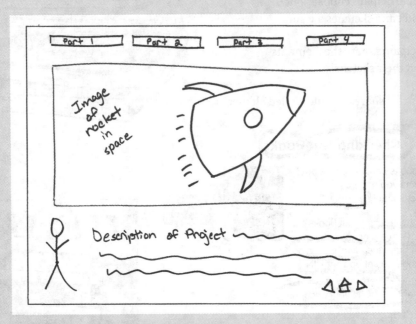

VISUAL LITERACY STANDARDS CONNECTION
- ACRL Visual Literacy Standard 6, Performance Indicator 2

Storyboard Template

Sketch out your design ideas in the boxes below. Use a separate box for each major segment of your project. Use the space below each sketch to add notes or other details to help you implement the project later.

1. Description: _____

_____

_____

2. Description: _____

_____

_____

3. Description: _____

_____

_____

4. Description: _____

_____

_____

Creating Graphical Representations of Data

LEARNING OUTCOME

- Construct graphic representations of data and information.

DESCRIPTION

Show students different types of graphical representations of data and discuss the purposes for which they can be used. These might include bar charts, pie charts, line charts, flow-charts, tree diagrams, and others. You may also want to show students ways that data are presented through infographics or review some of the elements and principles of design. For more information, see the "Visualizing Data" section in chapter 1, "Interpret and Analyze Images."

Distribute a collection of data to students (such as the accompanying examples) and ask them to work with a partner (or partners) to represent all or part of it using some kind of graphical representation. This activity can be done using technology, but it works just as well to have students sketch their representations.

Students can express data using a variety of representations, as are shown in the accompanying examples.

What percentage of students report that they are banned or discouraged from using their mobile devices in the classroom?

Example 1

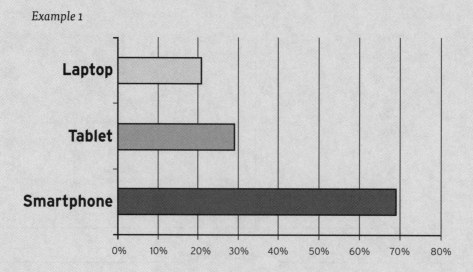

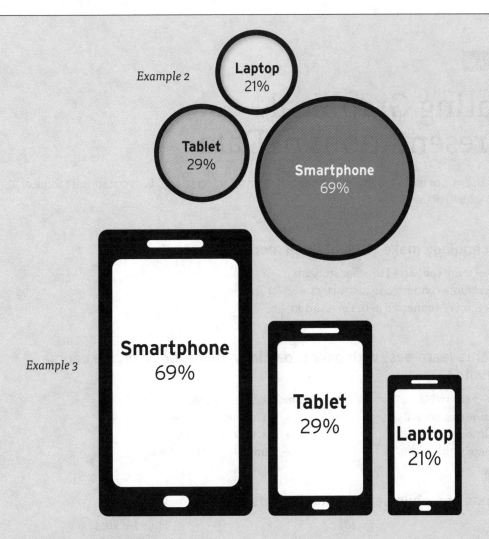

Example 2

Laptop
21%

Tablet
29%

Smartphone
69%

Example 3

Smartphone
69%

Tablet
29%

Laptop
21%

OPTIONAL EXTENSION

- Data in this activity are drawn from Educause's 2014 *ECAR Study of Undergraduate Students and Information Technology* and are depicted visually through an infographic online (http://net.educause.edu/ir/library/pdf/ss14/Eig1406.pdf). If you use these data (or other data drawn from an infographic), show students the image after they have completed the activity and ask them how their graphic representations compare.

TIPS FOR SUCCESS

- If students have access to technology, it might help to have students look at some of the chart options that are available in Word, PowerPoint, Excel, or another type of software.
- You can distribute a data set related to the course topic. Consider presenting students with different types (time-based data, percentages, etc.).
- As an alternative to distributing data, have students conduct a short survey to collect their own data about a topic or find a data set online.

VISUAL LITERACY STANDARDS CONNECTION

- ACRL Visual Literacy Standard 6, Performance Indicator 1

Creating Graphical Representations of Data

Directions: Use one or more graphical representations (you select which) to communicate some or all (you select which) of the following data.

Does technology make students feel more connected?

- 51% feel more connected to other students
- 54% feel more connected to instructors
- 65% feel more connected to the institution

Do students learn best with online, partially online, or no online course components?

Students 18–24 years old
- No online components: 19%
- Partially online: 75%
- Completely online: 6%

Students 25+ years old
- No online components: 15%
- Partially online: 66%
- Completely online: 19%

What kinds of mobile devices do students own?

2013
- Smartphones: 76%
- Tablets: 31%

2014
- Smartphones: 86%
- Tablets: 47%

Projected 2015
- Smartphones: 90%
- Tablets: 58%

Do students report that they are allowed to use their mobile devices in the classroom?

Banned/Discouraged
- Laptop: 21%
- Tablet: 29%
- Smartphone: 69%

Encouraged/Required
- Laptop: 25%
- Tablet: 15%
- Smartphone: 6%

Editing Images

LEARNING OUTCOMES

- Experiment with image editing tools to make changes to images.
- Evaluate the reliability of images as visual communications.

DESCRIPTION

Experimenting with image editing tools can help students see the method behind the magic of "Photoshopping." Select an image relevant to the course content, look at the metadata together, and discuss the meaning of the image. Working in pairs and using image editing software, students make one change to the original image and identify the implications.

DISCUSSION PROMPTS

- What was changed from the original photograph?
- Was the change obvious and easy to find, or did it blend in with the original?
- Has the meaning of the original image been changed through editing? How so?
- Going forward, looking at similar images related to the topic at hand, what will you look for and what questions will you ask?

TIP FOR SUCCESS

- Begin this activity by discussing alterations in popular media to help students make the connections between image editing and changed meanings.

OPTIONAL EXTENSION

- Use a variation of **Coffee Break! Edit an Image** in the classroom.

VISUAL LITERACY STANDARDS CONNECTION

- ACRL Visual Literacy Standard 6, Performance Indicators 3 and 4

Design Critique

LEARNING OUTCOME

- Employ a design critique framework to evaluate visual products.

DESCRIPTION

The design critique process is used for peer feedback in the visual arts. To run this activity, you will act as a facilitator. Timing this activity will help it go smoothly, and we have included "(___ minutes)" in each section for you to fill in your own times. For each visual product being critiqued, give participants a **Reflection Worksheet** and a **Design Critique Worksheet**.

To begin, everyone fills out the Reflection Worksheet (___ minutes). Explain that these reflection notes will become talking points for the critique. Then start the design critique process.

- *Round 1* (___ minutes): A presenter explains the goal of the work-in-progress and mentions any roadblocks or challenges. Participants record notes.
- *Round 2* (___ minutes): Participants critique the work by writing answers to the following questions: What is the *best* thing about this work? What is *one* recommendation you would make to improve this work? Facilitate a discussion that sticks to these questions.
- *Round 3* (___ minutes): After all participants have given feedback, allow the presenter to describe plans for incorporating the feedback into the work.

TIPS FOR SUCCESS

- Design critiques work best for works-in-progress because they generate feedback that can improve the work. Be sure to explain that the goal of the critique is to bring in new perspectives to make the work stronger—this approach builds trust between the facilitator and participants.
- Timing each round helps to focus attention and keep the critique fair.

VISUAL LITERACY STANDARDS CONNECTION

- ACRL Visual Literacy Standard 6, Performance Indicator 4

Reflection

Think about the work you are presenting today and answer the following questions. You will use these as talking points to present your work to your peers.

What is the goal of this work? What do you hope it communicates?

What roadblocks or challenges have you encountered?

Design Critique

Round 1: Listen to the presenter explain the goal of the work-in-progress and roadblocks. Record notes here:

Round 2: Critique the work by answering the following questions.

What is the best thing about this work?

_____

_____

_____

What is one recommendation you would make to improve this work?

_____

_____

_____

Round 3: After all participants have given feedback, listen to the presenter describe plans for incorporating the feedback into the work.

Ethical Use of Images

MAGES CARRY CORE cultural and personal expressions and information, packaged in an engaging format that is easy to use and share. This ease can raise challenging ethical issues in academic, personal, and—for librarians—professional realms. You've likely faced questions or dilemmas about using images ethically. Maybe you weren't sure what to say when you noticed a student assuming that every image online can be reused in a multimedia project. Or maybe a faculty member asked you to teach students to use images ethically, but you didn't have an activity you felt confident leading. Perhaps you've encountered an ethical conundrum of your own. Solutions aren't always simple or immediate, and the process of exploring ethical issues can be daunting. Complex concepts and new terminology can be barriers to making ethical choices about image use, while a focus on technical and legal issues can cause one to lose a broad ethical view.

A working knowledge of copyright and fair use is essential to an overall understanding of ethical image use. Copyright may be familiar territory, as you've worked with students to quote and paraphrase text, access electronic reserves and course materials, or contribute electronic theses or dissertations to an institutional repository. Images present questions about copyright that you may be less confident addressing and may have less practice dealing with. The lack of comfort with image-related copyright can inhibit scholars' effectiveness in a world where multimodal scholarship has become the norm. You can be a resource for students and faculty grappling with copyright and new media, and

ACTIVITIES IN THIS CHAPTER

facilitate an understanding of copyright and fair use that advances scholarship. You and your students will also want to know about new licensing models, such as Creative Commons, and the options available to you with open image content.

In this chapter we share basic information, tools, and resources for using images ethically and applying copyright effectively. For many of the topics covered here, there is not a clear right or wrong answer: the use of images involves judgment calls. As with other ethical issues in the scholarly communication process, choices about image use are best addressed with students through examples, discussion, and analytical exercises.

Foundational Questions

What Do I Need to Think about before I Use and Share Images?

Take a moment to consider copyright and ethics. Are you using an image someone else created? Will your image use impact other people? Think these questions through as you work with images in your academic projects and personal life.

What Copyright Specifics Apply to Images?

Update your knowledge of best practices around image copyright and licensing. What is a Creative Commons license? Is it okay to adapt an old painting in your new art project? Familiarize yourself with copyright basics and know what to look for in licenses and terms of use, and you'll be able to use images confidently in a variety of circumstances.

How Are Ethical Issues Relevant to My Image Use?

Ethical questions about image use crop up every day. You just posted a selfie, but a friend lets you know that she's unhappy that her face is visible in the background. Maybe you're working on a group project, and a collaborator wants to use an image that makes you feel uncomfortable. How do you figure out what to do? Understanding best practices will guide you toward an ethical course of action.

Are There Broader Societal Issues to Keep in Mind?

Creating, using, and sharing images can raise many societal issues in addition to personal questions of privacy and safety. What about image censorship? How does a society decide who is able to see what images, and when? Representations can reinforce stereotypes and biases. How do we incorporate diversity into our image choices? Images can be powerful, and social issues often include visual components worth critical thought.

Images and Copyright

With the steady stream of images flowing across our desktops and devices, it can be all too easy to forget that images can be intellectual property, like text, video, and music. Before sharing or reusing images, pause for a moment and figure out how image copyright applies to your situation. The goal of copyright law is to further scientific discovery, culture, and new scholarship. Copyright law affords rights to both creators and users in support of this goal. Keep this framework in mind as you delve into copyright questions, and the details and best practices will make more sense. Images, like text, video, music, and other formats, are covered by copyright. Image creators and users have the same rights as creators and users of other types of cultural and scientific production.

In this section, we take a close look at the key concepts related to image copyright, including fair use, public domain, licenses, and open content. Our **Copyright Basics** chart highlights additional need-to-know information related to image copyright and ethical use; **Activity 4.1: Understanding Image Copyright** presents the basics in a quiz format.

FAIR USE

Fair use provides rights to the public to use copyrighted works in some circumstances while protecting the rights of image creators. Fair use safeguards free expression and prevents owners' monopoly over transformative uses of their work. Examples of activities that rely on fair use include news reporting, criticism, parodies such as *Saturday Night Live,* teaching, and research. Copyright law outlines the four factors that determine whether a use is fair:

Factor 1: The purpose and character of the use, including whether the use is of a commercial nature or is for nonprofit educational purposes

Factor 2: The nature of the copyrighted work

Factor 3: The amount and substantiality of the portion used in relation to the copyrighted work as a whole

Factor 4: The effect of the use upon the potential market for, or value of, the copyrighted work

The four factors are used as a whole to determine fair use, and the relative importance of each factor varies according to the circumstances. Recently, courts have focused on two key questions that synthesize the four factors in deciding fair use. These questions focus on the idea of transformative use and on the amount of the original work used to achieve the transformative purpose:

- Did the use "transform" the material taken from the copyrighted work by using it for a broadly beneficial purpose different from that of the original, or did it just repeat the work for the same intent and value as the original?
- Was the material taken appropriate in kind and amount, considering the nature of the copyrighted work and of the use?

The four factors and key questions are a good place to start when analyzing whether your image use falls within fair use. But even with careful analysis, the best course of action is not always apparent. This lack of clarity often leads image users to unnecessarily err on the side of caution. Fortunately, communities across fields such as education, media, science, and the arts have developed codes of best practices to navigate and assess fair use as it applies to their common activities. Fair use best practices provide background, perspective, and vocabulary to illustrate the nuances of copyright and fair use through various professional and disciplinary lenses. As members of these communities embrace these codes, they clarify what fair use means in their work; over time, this activity reduces some of the ambiguities of fair use. Discover the fair use codes of best practices most relevant to image users listed in our **More to Explore: Fair Use Best Practices** feature. Use **Activity 4.2: Fair Use Debate** to help students think through fair use scenarios.

PUBLIC DOMAIN

Images in the public domain are free for all to use for any purpose. Some works originate in the public domain, such as most works created by the U.S. government and most works published in the United States prior to 1923. Copyright law sets a time limit on copyright, and works enter the public domain when their copyright expires. Creators can also release their work into the public domain. Try the tools and resources in **More to Explore: Copyright Tools** to determine whether a work may be in the public domain.

MORE TO EXPLORE: FAIR USE BEST PRACTICES

Code of Best Practices in Fair Use for Academic and Research Libraries (2012)

Who: Association of Research Libraries (ARL); Center for Social Media, School of Communication, American University; Program on Information Justice and Intellectual Property, Washington College of Law, American University

Focus: Accessing, storing, exhibiting, and providing access to copyrighted material

Code of Best Practices in Fair Use for the Visual Arts (2015)

Who: College Art Association (CAA), Patricia Aufderheide, Peter Jaszi

Focus: Using copyrighted materials for analytic writing about art, teaching about art, making art; providing online access to collections in memory institutions

Set of Principles in Fair Use for Journalism (2013)

Who: Society for Professional Journalists, Patricia Aufderheide, Peter Jaszi

Focus: Using copyrighted material as factual proof, for cultural criticism, to illustrate a news event, for historical reference, for generating public discussion of news, or to add value to evolving news

Statement on the Fair Use of Images for Teaching, Research, and Study (2011)

Who: Visual Resources Association (VRA), Gretchen Wagner, Allan T. Kohl

Focus: Preservation, using images for teaching purposes, using images for online study materials, creating adaptations of images for academic purposes, sharing images among educational and cultural institutions, and reproducing images in theses and dissertations

Documentary Filmmakers' Statement of Best Practices in Fair Use (2005)

Who: Association of Independent Video and Filmmakers; Independent Feature Project; International Documentary Association; National Alliance for Media Arts and Culture; Women in Film and Video, Washington, D.C., Chapter

Focus: Employing copyrighted materials for social or political critique, making an argument, or illustrating a historical sequence

MORE TO EXPLORE: COPYRIGHT TOOLS

Copyright Advisory Network: Resources

http://librarycopyright.net/resources

These tools from ALA's Office of Information Technology Policy include the Copyright Genie, the Fair Use Evaluator, the Public Domain Slider, and more. Access these tools directly or use the embed code to place them in a web page or research guide.

Copyright Services: Thinking Through Fair Use

www.lib.umn.edu/copyright/fairthoughts

This tool, developed by the University of Minnesota Libraries, uses a dynamic checklist to walk you through a fair use analysis.

Copyright Term and the Public Domain in the United States

https://copyright.cornell.edu/resources/publicdomain.cfm

This handy chart from Cornell University helps you determine the copyright terms for a work and determine whether a work is in the public domain.

TERMS OF USE AND LICENSE AGREEMENTS

Terms of use and license agreements are developed by image providers to define how the images they make available can be used. These terms and agreements supersede fair use and other copyright provisions. Using content provided under a license or terms of use typically implies your agreement to abide by that license or terms. Keep in mind that terms of use and license agreements may be more restrictive than fair use, so it is important to read and understand this information.

In online spaces, the terms of use may be located under an image or off to the side. You may have to click on a link that takes you to a page with this information. Terms of use may appear alongside Creative Commons language, a copyright symbol, or other indicators, depending on the rights status of the image. **Activity 4.3: Interpreting Terms of Use** provides an opportunity to practice looking at and interpreting terms of use statements for images. Of course, not all images are accompanied by terms of use or license agreements; use other strategies, such as a fair use analysis, to assess image availability in the absence of terms of use or a license.

Creative Commons

The nonprofit organization Creative Commons has developed a set of standard licenses that can be used with any work, including images. Creative Commons licenses simplify and streamline the process of sharing and using images and other content. Licenses are assigned by image creators themselves.

Creative Commons licenses are based on four basic elements that clearly indicate how works can be used, shared, and adapted. These elements are described in the **Creative Commons License Elements** chart. These elements can be used alone or combined to create different licenses for image creators to assign to their works. The licenses are indicated by a combination of their symbols and abbreviations. Because these licenses are written in simple language, reading them is a great way to understand the issues surrounding image copyright and sharing.

Creative Commons License Elements

SYMBOL	ABBREVIATION	TYPE	WHAT IT MEANS
(i)	BY	Attribution	You must give credit to the creator.
(S)	NC	NonCommercial	You cannot use the work to make money.
(=)	ND	No derivatives	You must use the work without altering it in any way.
(O)	SA	Share alike	You can alter the original work, as long as you share it under the same kind of license.

 COFFEE BREAK!

Choose a Creative Commons License

Identify an image that you created, or would like to create, and that you might consider using a Creative Commons license for. Briefly describe the image:

_____

Now use the Creative Commons License Chooser (http://creative commons.org/choose).

Is the license that the Chooser suggested the same one that you would choose? Read "About the Licenses" (https://creativecommons.org/licenses) to compare results.

How might you use this information in your work?

_____

_____

OPEN IMAGES

Open images are freely available online without restrictions on their use. Open media is an important component of open access in our contemporary academic environment of multimodal scholarship, teaching, and learning. Scholars increasingly need access to image content that they can reuse, reconfigure, and republish in open environments. Many cultural heritage institutions are embracing the values of open access and are providing unrestricted access to public domain works in their collections. Individuals are also assigning their work to the public domain by using tools such as the Creative Commons public domain mark or by contributing their work in spaces such as Wikimedia. We all now have many more options for accessing and using open image content than ever before.

Copyright Basics

Codes of best practices	Documents created by communities of practice to develop and recommend common practices and to help community members make informed decisions about copyright and fair use.
Copyright	Legal right of creators to control how their works are used by others. Images may be subject to multiple copyright claims, including claims by artists, photographers, designers, institutions, corporations, or others.
Copyright term	The period of time a work is covered by copyright. The copyright term is limited by copyright law.
Creative Commons	A nonprofit organization that offers a licensing system that provides a simplified way for people to share their work and identify how they permit others to build on and reuse it.
Educational use	Use in educational contexts or that directly relates to educational pursuits.
Fair use	A provision in copyright law that allows for the use of copyrighted works under some specific circumstances and for particular purposes such as criticism, comment, scholarship, or research.
Intellectual property	The products and results of creative or intellectual work, including designs, images, symbols, art, and architecture.
License agreement	An agreement between content providers or owners and users that determines how the content can be accessed and used. License agreements can be more restrictive than standard copyright provisions.
Open access (OA)	Content made freely available online without restrictions on access or use.

Open images	Images made available online without restrictions on distribution or reuse.
Public domain	Works not covered by copyright (because the copyright term has expired, the creator has released the work, or the work was never copyrighted) are in the public domain. The public then holds the rights to the work.
Restricted images	Images available only through payment or license systems, or images available only for specified restricted uses.
Terms of use	Descriptions of how particular databases, resources, or the images in them may be used.
Transformative use	A consideration used by the courts to evaluate fair use; refers to changes made to the original work, commentary, or value added.

Ethical Considerations of Image Use

You've likely heard news stories about lapses in judgment involving over-zealous selfie snapping or unintended image sharing. Technology makes it possible for anyone to create and share images with relative ease and speed, which can contribute to sharing images without much prior thought about the potential impact. This section examines ethical considerations around image use, from recognizing the impact of altering images to balancing your rights with the rights of others when taking photos in the public sphere. An awareness of image censorship brings a broader perspective to these ethical issues, as does mindfulness of the relationship between our personal biases and how we see images.

IMAGE ALTERATION

Image editing technologies make it easy for students to alter and share images in new contexts. The alteration of existing images can lead to products of creative expression that represent new meanings and present new information. However, altering images can also drastically transform the meanings of images in ways that may be unintended. Presenting an image in a new context can also dramatically alter its meaning. For example, an image of a child smelling a flower in a field has one meaning if used in an ad for a summer educational program but another meaning if used in an ad by a nonprofit organization raising money for children who are victims of war. Students need to consider carefully how the meaning of an image can change when the image or its context is altered. Chapter 1, "Interpret and Analyze Images," delves into approaches for careful looking and informed image interpretation.

PRIVACY AND PHOTOGRAPHY

Public photography is woven into the fabric of our daily life experiences and informs our knowledge and conceptualization of history. From Henri Cartier-Bresson's photos on the streets of Paris and Helen Levitt's photos of children in New York City to contemporary street photographer Eric Kim's work, photography provides a medium for vibrant artistic expression and crucial social documentation. Public photography has been a catalyst for social change, from photojournalist James "Spider" Martin's photos of the civil rights movement in the 1960s to present-day social strife, abuses of power, and civil rights violations, often captured by ordinary citizens.

In the United States, it is a constitutional right to take photos of anything in plain sight in public places. The American Civil Liberties Union's "Know Your Rights: Photographers" guides citizens through this right. Students will find this information helpful if they have an interest in street photography, social justice, or just taking photos on their phones when out and about. The National Press Photographers Association (NPPA) Code of Ethics guides visual journalists through the ethical considerations of taking public photographs, but private citizens will find these recommendations useful too. Guidelines include acting with consideration and compassion toward others, representing subjects honestly and without manipulation, and avoiding private moments of grief. The NPPA Code of Ethics is a useful conversation starter for the ethics and value of public photography.

Private photography is a different circumstance and can present challenges for students as they move between public and private environments. Private photography involves additional responsibility to the people in the photo, and it is important to consider their privacy preferences. A photo may start out as private, but once it is shared online it can be distributed and used in unanticipated ways. Because photos can contain a great deal of identifying information, they have the potential to compromise people's safety and well-being when made public. Comments made about images online can be problematic, harming reputations or injuring a person's dignity. Encouraging students to have conversations with each other about online image sharing can help raise awareness of potential pitfalls. **Activity 4.4: The Ethics of Image Sharing** provides an opportunity to develop sensitivity to privacy concerns and the implications of image sharing by working through case studies.

MORE TO EXPLORE: IMAGE ETHICS

Index on Censorship

www.indexoncensorship.org

An international organization that works to expose and raise awareness of attacks on free speech and artistic expression.

Know Your Rights: Photographers

www.aclu.org/know-your-rights/photographers

The American Civil Liberties Union's guide to taking photos in public places.

NPAA Code of Ethics

https://nppa.org/code_of_ethics

A code for visual journalists that serves as "an educational tool both for those who practice and for those who appreciate photojournalism."

Photographers Without Borders

www.photographerswithoutborders.org/ethical-photography

Guidelines intended to preserve the rights and dignity of the people whose images are captured.

CENSORSHIP

Librarians are accustomed to thinking about censorship in the context of banned books and free speech. The American Library Association is a strong proponent of the First Amendment and supports initiatives related to the freedom of the press and the freedom to read, including Banned Books Week and Choose Privacy Week. Image censorship involves a similar set of concerns, although images and image censorship can take on additional immediacy and intensity in public life. Like the censorship of written materials, image censorship can have profound implications for individual expression, equality, access to information, and social justice.

Events reported in the news highlight issues involving image censorship. For example, image censorship in social media can expose gender bias. As Jenna Wortham described in the *New York Times* in 2015, artist Rupi Kaur posted on Instagram fully clothed images of herself with menstrual stains on her clothing. Kaur's photos were immediately taken down after a complaint, while sexually charged images of bikini-clad women on spring break remained ubiquitous. A similar incident involved Facebook and images of women breast-feeding, as reported in a 2014 BBC piece titled "Mother Labelled 'Tramp' for Breastfeeding in Public." Art and religion are other targets for image censorship. In 2015, Slate.com reported that after the attacks on Charlie Hebdo in Paris, the Associated Press took down from its website images of "Piss Christ" by Andres Serrano, a work of art with a long history of controversy and censorship. Media reports about acts of war have also involved image censorship. In 2014, the *New York Post* published a front-page image of journalist James Foley, moments before he was beheaded by ISIS. Other media outlets called this "appalling" and condemned the *New York Post* for this "outrageous" image. The Twitter CEO warned Twitter users that their accounts would be suspended if they reposted this "graphic imagery."

Librarians need to be prepared to encourage student discourse on image censorship and be able to provide resources, information, and critical approaches to thinking about this issue. Any of the preceding cases provide a springboard for discussing image censorship with students. The nonprofit Index on Censorship is also a useful resource. An effective approach can be to present a case and a news article about it, ask students to discuss, then play a video or commentary that offers broader perspectives and additional discussion questions, such as David Greene's August 2014 NPR interview with David Hernandez, assistant professor at USC Annenberg, about censorship, images, and technology. Students can then resume their discussion, noting any aspects they hadn't considered previously.

REPRESENTATION AND DIVERSITY

How are people of different backgrounds, cultures, and identities represented in contemporary culture? How do we perceive those who are different from ourselves, based on the typical images we see of CEOs, firefighters, homeless people, doctors, or single mothers? A recent study of search results retrieved by Google Images suggests that stereotypical representations of occupations, for instance, are reinforced and exacerbated by the images we see in search results (Kay, Matuszek, and Munson 2015).

What can we do to counteract these stereotypes and broaden our picture of others? How can our personal image and viewing choices work toward social change, inclusion, and diversity? Research suggests that we can take action in our everyday lives to neutralize visual stereotypes and expand our ideas about what other people look like (Banaji and Greenwald 2013). It turns out that surrounding ourselves with images that are inconsistent with images we might typically see can diversify our conceptions of other people, act against our biases, and expand our understanding of other people and diversity.

COFFEE BREAK!

Change Your Screensaver

In *Blindspot: Hidden Biases of Good People,* Mahzarin Banaji and Anthony Greenwald (2013) suggest that the simple act of changing your screensaver to an image that works against stereotypes can help reset your biases. Banaji and Greenwald give the example of an image of a construction worker breast-feeding a baby.

Consider a personal bias about other people you may want to revise.

Find an image that counteracts this bias, and set it as your screensaver.

Next week, reflect on this image and its effect on your perceptions of others.

Next Steps

Ethical image use requires a broad understanding of the intellectual property landscape. To develop your skills in this area, try the following:

- Familiarize yourself with the resources highlighted in this chapter.
- Read various terms of use and license agreements to become familiar with how usage restrictions are commonly presented.
- Consider sharing your own images or assigning a Creative Commons license.

REFERENCES

Banaji, Mahzarin R., and Anthony G. Greenwald. 2013. *Blindspot: Hidden Biases of Good People.* New York: Delacorte.

Kay, Matthew, Cynthia Matuszek, and Sean A. Munson. 2015. "Unequal Representation and Gender Stereotypes in Image Search Results for Occupations." In *Proceedings of the 33rd Annual ACM Conference on Human Factors in Computing Systems,* 3819–28. New York: ACM.

Ethical Image Use Checklists

Work through these checklists to address the ethical concerns associated with reusing images or producing and sharing your own.

FOR AN IMAGE CREATED BY SOMEONE ELSE

Explore context.

- ☐ Identify the image source. Who is giving you access to this image and why?
- ☐ Identify who produced the image. What else do you know about this creator?
- ☐ Consider how the meaning of the image is affected by the context in which it appears. Does it appear elsewhere, and what does it mean there?

Notice and record details.

- ☐ Read terms of use, license agreements, and other use guidelines.
- ☐ Record the image title or caption, creator, date, source, and URL.
- ☐ Generate a citation or credit line.

Evaluate and make decisions.

- ☐ Determine if your intended use is permitted by the license or covered under fair use.
- ☐ Consider issues of privacy, safety, and the rights of others.
- ☐ Identify image manipulations you need to disclose to your audience, if relevant. Determine the best way to make this disclosure.

FOR AN IMAGE THAT YOU CREATE

Clarify your rights.

- ☐ Decide if and where you want to share your image.
- ☐ Determine how you want others to be able to use your work.
- ☐ If sharing, assign a Creative Commons license or create your own rights statement so others know whether and how they can use your work.

Address the rights of others.

- ☐ If required, seek consent of people in your images. Use a release form if appropriate.
- ☐ If required, cite or credit the work of others that you have built on.

Consider broader ethical issues.

- ☐ Double-check your use of others' work. Reread the rights statement or review your fair use analysis.
- ☐ If required, disclose your image alterations or manipulations.
- ☐ Respect the privacy and dignity rights of others when distributing or sharing images.

ACTIVITY 4.1

Understanding Image Copyright

LEARNING OUTCOMES

- Navigate intellectual property and copyright issues related to image use.
- Reflect on personal experience with intellectual property issues.

DESCRIPTION

Prior to conducting this activity, provide students with information about image copyright, fair use, Creative Commons, and privacy. Students complete the **Image Copyright Knowledge Check Worksheet** individually or with a partner, or you can incorporate the questions into a class presentation and ask students to volunteer the answers. See the **Answer Key** for the answers.

TIPS FOR SUCCESS

- Consider asking students to share personal experiences that the questions bring to mind.
- Share your own experiences—do any of the questions resonate with you?
- Deliver the questions with an anonymous poll or survey, then discuss the answers.

OPTIONAL EXTENSION

- Create bingo cards using the image copyright–related vocabulary from this chapter. To play the game, students check vocabulary mentioned during discussion.

VISUAL LITERACY STANDARDS CONNECTION

- ACRL Visual Literacy Standard 7, Performance Indicator 1

Image Copyright Knowledge Check

1. Images that are available online can be reused for any purpose.

   A. True   B. False

2. If an image is in the public domain, you can use it in a paper or project without citing it.

   A. True   B. False

3. To obtain copyright for a photo you took, you need to file paperwork with the U.S. Copyright Office.

   A. True   B. False

4. You are creating a web page and want to include a photograph that you took at a party. The photo contains close-ups of other people. Is it ethical to use this photograph?

   A. Yes, I took it, so it is my photograph to do with as I wish.
   B. Yes, if the people in the photograph explicitly say it is okay.
   C. No, I can only post photos of myself, my family, and inanimate objects.

5. You are creating a video and want to incorporate a Creative Commons photo with an Attribution-NonCommercial 4.0 license. Under what conditions can you use the photo and distribute your video?

   A. You can use the photo as long as you cite or credit it.
   B. You can use the photo as long as you cite or credit it and do not use it in a commercial enterprise.
   C. You can use the photo as long as you share your video under a Creative Commons license.

6. To use a Creative Commons photo, you need to read and follow the license, but nothing else.

   A. True   B. False

7. All of the following are elements seen in Creative Commons licenses except:

   A. No Derivatives   C. No Sharing
   B. Attribution   D. NonCommercial

8. Which of the following is not one of the four factors of fair use?

   A. Effect on the potential market   C. Purpose and character of use
   B. Nature of the work   D. Creator of the work

9. Which of the following best represents a transformative use?

   A. Reposting on your website a cute photo of a puppy you found on the Internet
   B. In an academic research paper, analyzing (and reproducing) images from the media used to raise awareness of human trafficking
   C. Changing the colors on a data graph you found in a research article
   D. Changing a word in a meme you found on BuzzFeed and reposting it

Answer Key: Image Copyright Knowledge Check

1. **False.** Availability on the Web does not necessarily mean availability for reuse. Check the terms of use, Creative Commons license, or other rights statements before you reuse an image you find on the Web. The image is there for you to view in context but not necessarily for you to reuse.

2. **False.** Public domain images are available for any use by anyone, but you still need to cite images you use that are not your own work.

3. **False.** Copyright is yours when you create something new; no need to file paperwork. Now what will you do with that? Consider whether you want to share your image and what you want others to be able to do with it.

4. **B.** Yes, if the people in the photograph explicitly say it is fine with them. Some people may object to having their image posted in online spaces, so be sure to check. Most professional organizations have people sign a release form to give permission.

5. **B.** You can use and distribute the photo as long as you cite or credit it and do not make money from your video or use it in a commercial enterprise. There are different types of Creative Commons licenses, so read the license to determine how you can use the image.

6. **True.** Creative Commons licenses tell you everything you need to know about whether and how you can use the image. Read the license carefully, follow all provisions, and you're set! The goal of Creative Commons is to make reuse simple.

7. **C.** "No Sharing" never appears in Creative Commons licenses. Rather, "Share Alike" is an element of many.

8. **D.** "Creator of the work" is not one of the four factors. The fourth factor is the amount and substantiality of the portion used.

9. **B.** In an academic research paper, including and analyzing images in the media raising awareness of human trafficking. Commentary is usually considered to be a transformative use. Be sure to cite the original images to give credit and so others can investigate these sources themselves. Choice D might also be transformative, depending on the word you change. Investigate the meme, where it came from, and how it was created. Did your single word change create an entirely new meaning? If so, you might be within fair use guidelines.

Fair Use Debate

LEARNING OUTCOMES

- Analyze the four factors of fair use with real-world cases.
- Discuss and apply the two transformative use questions.

DESCRIPTION

Introduce the concept of fair use and present the two transformative use questions. Give students a worksheet describing one or two selected cases that concern fair use, such as *Cariou v. Prince* (Case Study 1) and Shepard Fairey's Obama "Hope" poster (Case Study 2) in the **Fair Use Debate Worksheet**. Have students review selected cases in consideration of the four factors and transformative use as a whole. Show students the images in question. Then ask students, "Do you think the artist who used the image can claim fair use?" Consider using the Fair Use Evaluator (http://librarycopyright.net/resources/fairuse) or the Thinking Through Fair Use (https://www.lib.umn.edu/copyright/fairthoughts) tool to walk through the analysis. During discussion, ask students to share their reasoning. Then present the outcomes of the cases. Were there differences of opinion? Why?

TIP FOR SUCCESS

- Keep in mind that the four-factor test is applied case-by-case by federal judges, so there are no definitive answers outside the courts. Copyright infringement cases are often settled between the parties, leaving the fair use issue unresolved. Because it is open-ended, the fair use doctrine presents challenges to teachers, students, content creators, and even the judges who apply it. Nevertheless, teaching our students to grapple with the flexible nature of fair use encourages them to see themselves as citizens in a shared, participatory culture with the responsibility to make well-informed decisions regarding the use of others' intellectual property and their own.

OPTIONAL EXTENSION

- Ask students to reflect upon and share their own stories and experiences related to fair use.

VISUAL LITERACY STANDARDS CONNECTION

- ACRL Visual Literacy Standard 7, Performance Indicator 1

The Fair Use Debate

CASE STUDY 1: CARIOU V. PRINCE

Richard Prince's series of paintings "Canal Zone" (2008) used thirty-five images from French photographer Patrick Cariou's book *Yes, Rasta* (2000). In 2009 Cariou sued Prince, New York's Gagosian Gallery and its owner, and the catalog publisher for copyright infringement. In March 2011, U.S. District Judge Deborah Batts ruled against Prince on the basis that his paintings did not transform the photographs in a way that commented on the originals. That decision was largely overturned by the Second Circuit Court of Appeals in April 2013, with the exception of five paintings that were to be reevaluated for claims of fair use. However, both parties settled the suit and voluntarily dismissed the action.

Do you think that Prince can claim fair use? Why or why not? _____

_____

_____

Do you think Prince's use of Cariou's photographs was transformative? Why or why not? _____

_____

_____

What other information would help you decide? _____

_____

_____

CASE STUDY 2: SHEPARD FAIREY'S OBAMA "HOPE" POSTER

Street artist Shepard Fairey created the Obama "Hope" campaign poster in 2008, first claiming that he based it on a cropped photograph of Obama with actor George Clooney. Fairey later revealed that he had used a photograph taken by Associated Press photographer Mannie Garcia. The civil lawsuit *Fairey v. The Associated Press* was settled by the two parties and therefore never judged by a court on the terms of fair use.

Do you think that Fairey can claim fair use? Why or why not? _____

_____

_____

Do you think Fairey's use of the AP photograph was transformative? Why or why not? _____

_____

_____

What other information would help you decide? _____

_____

_____

Interpreting Terms of Use

LEARNING OUTCOMES

- Develop familiarity with how terms of use statements are presented.
- Practice interpreting terms of use in different contexts.

DESCRIPTION

Show students several examples of images in different websites or image databases and show them how to navigate to the terms of use and copyright information. Look closely at the terms of use from Creative Commons, NASA, and the Library of Congress, and work as a class to interpret what they mean. If it would be helpful for your students, print out copies of the terms of use texts.

Students work in pairs or small groups to find two images on their own and locate the terms of use associated with those images. Students then complete the **Interpreting Terms of Use Worksheet** to record what they are permitted to do with the images that they find, according to the associated terms of use.

TIPS FOR SUCCESS

- Prior to conducting this activity, provide students with basic information about copyright, terms of use, and Creative Commons licenses.
- This activity is best done in pairs or small groups so that students can help each other interpret the terms of use for different images.

VISUAL LITERACY STANDARDS CONNECTION

- ACRL Visual Literacy Standard 7, Performance Indicators 1 and 2

Interpreting Terms of Use

Find two images using different image sources—Flickr, NASA, or Library of Congress American Memory. Locate the terms of use and answer the following questions.

Image 1

Source used: _____

Image title: _____

License restrictions: _____

- If Creative Commons, which license type? _____

- If in the public domain, how do you know? _____

- If "All Rights Reserved," how do you know? _____

Explore the license or terms of use and check each box that applies.

For this image, I am permitted to:

☐ Download it.

☐ Post it to a website.

☐ Use it for commercial purposes.

☐ Use it for a class presentation.

☐ Modify it.

If I use this image, I must:

☐ Provide attribution to the creator.

☐ Include a link to the license.

☐ Provide a credit line.

I still have questions about:

_____

_____

_____

Interpreting Terms of Use

Find two images using different image sources—Flickr, NASA, or Library of Congress American Memory. Locate the terms of use and answer the following questions.

| Image 2 |

Source used: _____

Image title: _____

License restrictions: _____

- If Creative Commons, which license type? _____

- If in the public domain, how do you know? _____

- If "All Rights Reserved," how do you know? _____

Explore the license or terms of use and check each box that applies.

For this image, I am permitted to:

☐ Download it.

☐ Post it to a website.

☐ Use it for commercial purposes.

☐ Use it for a class presentation.

☐ Modify it.

If I use this image, I must:

☐ Provide attribution to the creator.

☐ Include a link to the license.

☐ Provide a credit line.

I still have questions about:

_____

_____

_____

The Ethics of Image Sharing

LEARNING OUTCOME

- Explore issues related to ethics, privacy, and etiquette with case studies about the online sharing of images.

DESCRIPTION

Small groups examine one of the scenarios listed in the **Ethics of Image Sharing Worksheet**. Students discuss the scenario with their group members and answer the related question(s). After groups discuss each scenario, review the scenarios as a class using the discussion prompts. Ask groups to explain their rationale.

All scenarios are inspired by incidents reported in the news and are constructed with fictitious names for ease of use in teaching and learning. The following are some of the topics that you may want to discuss with students regarding each scenario.

Scenario 1: Maria and Jada

This scenario is inspired by a question posted to Amy Dickinson's column in the *Tulsa World* on January 28, 2013, called "Is Posting Friend's Photo on Facebook a Double Standard?"

Who owns the photo—Maria or Jada? Should Maria have removed the photo? Should she repost it?

> *Maria may own the photo, but Jada has a right to ask that a picture of herself be removed from the Internet, and Maria should comply. Even if Jada has posted other pictures of herself, she has a right to object to a particular photo.*

Scenario 2: Russell, Kim, and Miguel

This scenario is inspired by a legal case in Singapore involving blogger Wendy Cheng, also known as Xiaxue. The story was reported in the *Straits Times* (Singapore) on June 9, 2012.

Does Kim have a case? Should Russell have posted the photos of Kim and Miguel on his blog?

> *Russell does not own the rights to the photos or have permission to post the photos of his critics; therefore, Russell does not have the right to repost the photos on his blog.*

Scenario 3: Althea and Jamal

This scenario is inspired by an article by Tatiana Boncompagni, a New York–based author and journalist. Her story, "Whose Picture Is It, Anyway?," appeared on the *New York Times* website on April 11, 2014, and in print on April 13, 2014.

Should Althea have posted the photos over her son's objections? Why or why not?

Althea can post the photos because she is Jamal's parent, but she should respect her son's wish (which is not unreasonable) and refrain from posting the photos.

Scenario 4: Ayesha and Miranda

This scenario is inspired by a piece featured on CBS Boston on November 20, 2012, called "Facebook Photo of Plymouth Woman at Tomb of the Unknowns Sparks Outrage."

Should Ayesha resign from her job? Why or why not?

What Ayesha did was disrespectful, and her actions had repercussions that she did not anticipate.

TIPS FOR SUCCESS

- Rather than reviewing the "rules" of online posting before discussing the scenarios, have students discuss the scenarios without prior instruction so that they can work through some of these issues on their own.
- As you discuss the scenarios, help students make a distinction between behavior that is technically legal and behavior that may not be ethical, courteous, or safe.
- Encourage students to make connections to their own experience. For example, most of these issues discuss images posted on Facebook, but to what other types of situations do they apply?

OPTIONAL EXTENSIONS

- Present students with other current news stories about issues related to image sharing and ask students to discuss their reactions.
- Instruct students to find a news story related to image sharing in online spaces. Ask students to summarize the story for the class and discuss the issues.

VISUAL LITERACY STANDARDS CONNECTION

- ACRL Visual Literacy Standard 7, Performance Indicator 1

The Ethics of Image Sharing

SCENARIO 1: MARIA AND JADA

After getting married, Maria posted her wedding photos on her Facebook page. The photos included different shots of the guests enjoying themselves at the reception. After seeing these pictures, Jada, one of the guests, contacted Maria and asked her to remove a photo that Jada was in, saying that she didn't like having her photo posted online. Maria complied with Jada's request and removed the photo. Later, Maria looked up Jada on Facebook and saw that Jada did indeed have a Facebook account of her own. Not only did Jada have an account, but she had posted lots of photos of herself and her family on her Facebook page! Maria felt irritated that Jada had asked her to remove a photo, when Jada clearly didn't object to having other photos of herself posted online.

Who owns the photo—Maria or Jada? Should Maria have removed the photo? Should she repost it?

_____

_____

_____

_____

_____

SCENARIO 2: RUSSELL, KIM, AND MIGUEL

Russell is a college student who has a Facebook page and maintains a blog. Two other students, Kim and Miguel, made fun of Russell's blog on Facebook. To retaliate, Russell copied Kim's and Miguel's photos from their Facebook pages and posted them on his blog, with commentary about why Kim and Miguel were wrong. He also made fun of their appearances. When Kim saw the blog post with her picture, she demanded that Russell take down her photo, saying that he did not have a right to post her picture. Russell refused, saying that Kim had posted her photo on Facebook and that it was free to be reposted on other sites. Kim objected and threatened to sue the blog owner.

Does Kim have a case? Should Russell have posted the photos of Kim and Miguel on his blog?

_____

_____

_____

_____

_____

SCENARIO 3: ALTHEA AND JAMAL

While on vacation with her family, Althea took some photos of her husband and two kids. Althea showed the pictures to her children and told them that she planned to post the pictures on her Facebook page. Her eight-year-old son, Jamal, objected, saying that he didn't want her to post his picture. When Althea asked him why, he said that too many people could see it and he found it embarrassing. Althea told her son that there was absolutely nothing embarrassing about the photos, but he was not convinced. Althea thought that her friends would enjoy seeing them, so she decided to post them anyway.

Should Althea have posted the photos over her son's objections? Why or why not?

_____

_____

_____

_____

_____

_____

SCENARIO 4: AYESHA AND MIRANDA

While on a business trip in Washington, D.C., Ayesha and her friend Miranda visited Arlington National Cemetery. The two saw a sign saying "Silence and Respect" that stood near the Tomb of the Unknowns. Because they were having fun, Miranda took a picture of Ayesha appearing to shout and raising her middle finger next to the sign. Ayesha thought it was funny and posted the photo on her Facebook page. News of the photo quickly spread, and many people were angered by her disrespect. One person even created a Facebook page demanding that Ayesha be fired from her job. The incident resulted in bad publicity for the company where Ayesha worked, and she was asked to resign. Ayesha said that she was just having fun and meant no disrespect.

Should Ayesha resign from her job? Why or why not?

_____

_____

_____

_____

_____

_____

Cite and Credit Images

YOU'VE FOUND THAT great image! Now what? You'll need to cite or credit the image when you use it, and this chapter will help you do it right. Citing images is a fundamental part of using images in academic work, but it remains a source of confusion and anxiety for students, faculty, and many of us working with them. Style guides do not always provide complete or extensive discussion or examples of image citations, and citation generation and management tools are geared more for text materials. So you're often left to piece together a best-guess approach.

The broad range of contexts in which students use images also presents challenges for citing and crediting images appropriately. Of course images need to be cited in research papers, but what about posters or creative work? What is the best way to credit an image online? In this chapter, we explore these questions and more, and we offer examples and activities for modeling and practicing image citations. You will deepen your understanding of why we cite images, build confidence for citing and crediting images in a variety of contexts, and open discussion about how image citation can advance creative work and engagement with visual materials.

ACTIVITIES IN THIS CHAPTER

Foundational Questions

Am I Using an Image Someone Else Created?

Use images created by other people deliberately and thoughtfully. If you're using someone else's image in your work, remember that you'll always need to cite or credit it.

Why Do I Need to Cite an Image?

Cite images others create in order to give credit to the creator, to provide information so others can find and reuse the image, and to participate in ongoing scholarly conversations.

Where Do I Find Information to Create a Citation?

Explore the caption and text around the image, reference lists, and links. It can take detective work to find all the information you need!

What Is the Best Way to Cite an Image in My Project?

You can provide a citation or a credit, depending on your project and where and how you are using the image. Know your options and best practices.

How Do I Format the Citation?

Use the citation style recommended by your instructor, and follow our tips for citing images in different contexts.

Why Cite Images?

Have you ever come across an image and wondered where it originated? Or have you tried to use an image for a project, and then realized the image might not be from the same time period as your research topic? Or maybe you needed to refer to an image when discussing it, but couldn't find a title. Citing images heads off these problems by providing the information we need to engage in conversations about visual materials.

Understanding image citation best practices helps us to ethically and productively use images others create, which in turn advances discussion and inquiry. Citing images in academic work acknowledges the work of others and provides information about the image so it can be identified, understood, and evaluated by your readers or audience.

Build familiarity with common image citation practices across disciplines and the information typically included in citations by looking for image credits or citations in research and study materials. Closely examining image citations also gives context and meaning to images and can expose gaps in information provided, prompting further research. The activities in this chapter provide an opportunity to apply citation practices and to discuss when and why to cite images. **Activity 5.1: Why Cite Images?** provides prompts to open a discussion about images in the scholarly communication process.

Formulating Image Citations, Credits, and Captions

Gathering all the necessary information for an image citation can involve some sleuthing. Captions, credits, and citations may not provide all the information you need to reuse and cite an image. You may need to read the text surrounding an image, inspect a website address, check a list of illustrations in a book, interpret tags, or deploy strategies such as reverse image searching. In **Activity 5.2: Gathering Information for Image Citations**, practice looking at the text that accompanies images to figure out the key information needed for generating citations and credits.

Once you have found all the relevant information about your image, you will need to formulate your image citation, credit, or caption. How you format the citation and where it appears depends on the type of project. Online image credits are structured differently than image citations in an academic paper's reference list, for example. Use the **Citing and Crediting Practices by Project Type** chart to help you decide how and where to cite or credit the images you are using.

Citing and Crediting Practices by Project Type

TYPE OF PROJECT	LOCATION OF CITATION OR CREDIT	STYLE AND TIPS
Research paper	Reference list and figure or caption	Academic citation style Use a standard citation style such as APA or MLA. Use the style recommended by your instructor. Use the same style for images that you use for other research materials such as books and articles.
Poster	Caption directly under each image or brief caption and reference list	Adapted academic citation style Format captions or reference list citations following standard citation style guidelines. Consider the overall style and appearance of your poster when deciding whether to use captions or a reference list. Citation information may be more appropriate or visually appealing in one location or the other. Image credits should appear on the front of the poster with the images, not on the back of the poster where they cannot be seen or in a separate handout.

(continued)

TYPE OF PROJECT	LOCATION OF CITATION OR CREDIT	STYLE AND TIPS
Presentation	Caption directly under each image or in an images list at the end of your presentation	Adapted academic citation style
		Format captions or images list following standard citation style guidelines.
		Consider the overall style and visual impact of your presentation when deciding whether to use captions or an images list. Citation information may be more appropriate or visually appealing in one location or the other.
Online space	Caption directly under image	Image credit with title, creator, date, link to source, and license or copyright information if relevant.
Creative work	Caption accompanying the image	Image credit with information about the new work and any reused images created by others.

CITING IMAGES IN ACADEMIC STYLES

Citing images in an academic style can be confusing if you're accustomed to citing primarily text sources. APA (American Psychological Association) and MLA (Modern Language Association) are two of the most common citation styles that students are asked to use. The *Publication Manual of the American Psychological Association* (6th edition) and the *MLA Handbook for Writers of Research Papers* (7th edition) provide some guidance for image citation, but they contain a limited number of examples and do not account for the variety of image types and the contexts in which images may appear. In this section, we bring together image-related citation guidelines dispersed throughout the citation manuals. We suggest best practices and models for citing the types of images and sources most commonly encountered by students and faculty.

Citing Images in APA Style

In-Text Citations

When citing images in APA style in the text of a paper, the creator's last name and the date of creation of the image are included in parentheses after the cited material, like this: (Creator, 1990). If there is no creator, a title can be used instead: (*Title*, 1990). If there is no title, use whatever information comes first in the complete citation in the reference list. Each in-text citation should clearly correspond to an item in the reference list.

Figures and Captions

In APA style, images are referred to as *figures* and can include graphs, charts, maps, drawings, and photographs. All images that are reproduced in a paper should be labeled as Figure 1, Figure 2, Figure 3, and so on. Tables are labeled as Table 1, Table 2, Table 3, and so on.

Figures are placed as close to their reference in the text as possible, with figure labels placed below the figure, followed by a brief explanatory caption. If you've created the figure yourself, a caption you create is sufficient. If using an image someone else created, include the complete citation information in the caption and in the reference list. Use the words "Retrieved from" prior to the source URL. Include institution credit line information before the "Retrieved from" information, if required by the museum or archive.

APA image captions generally follow this pattern:

> *Figure 1.* Author, A. A. (Year). *Title of material.* [Description of material]. Retrieved from http://www.xxxx

The following example shows how an image would be referenced in the text and in the caption.

Example: APA Figure Reference in the Text

Sargent's *Egyptians Raising Water from the Nile* demonstrates the atmospheric qualities apparent in his later works (see Figure 1).

Example: APA Figure Caption

Figure 1. Sargent, J. S. *Egyptians Raising Water from the Nile* [Painting]. 1890–91. The Metropolitan Museum of Art, Gift of Mrs. Francis Ormond, 1950 (50.130.16). Retrieved from www.metmuseum.org/collection/the-collection-online/search/12074

Reference List

Some variation exists in how images are cited in the references, depending on where the images are found. However, APA image citations generally follow this pattern:

> Creator, C. (Year of production or publication). *Title of work* [Description, Medium, or other relevant information]. Retrieval information or location of the work.

Figure 5.1 breaks down the different parts of an APA entry for an image found online, as it would appear in the reference list.

U.S Census Bureau. (2011, May 24). *Mississippi River: Significant flood outlook area* [Map]. Retrieved from http://www2.census.gov/geo/maps/special/MississippiRiverArea/MSRiverFlood_RefMap_052411.pdf.

Figure 5.1. *Parts of an image citation in the APA reference list*

The **Elements of APA Citations** chart describes these citation elements in more detail for a variety of image types and sources.

Elements of APA Citations

ELEMENT	CITATION FORMAT
Creator or producer	The creator's name is listed as Last name, First initial(s). If there is no individual creator, an organization may be used instead. If no creator or organization is available, then the title begins the citation. When citing an image found online, use the proper name of the creator if available; however, if only a screen name is available, use that instead.
Year of production or publication	If no date is available, n.d. should be used instead. If necessary, a date range may be used (1990-1992) or the abbreviation ca. can be used to indicate an approximate date (ca. 1956).
Title and format of image	The title of a stand-alone image is italicized; if the image is part of a larger work, then the image title should not be italicized and the name of the complete work should be included in italics. The title should be followed by the format in brackets, such as [Photograph], [Print], [Map], or [Sculpture]. If no title is available, then a description of the image may be used and should be placed in brackets.

(continued)

Other repository, publication, or production information	If the image was found on a website, list the URL; if the image was found in a subscription database, list the name of the database. If the image was from a museum or archive website, include any additional information the institution requires, such as the institution's name. For a museum or archive image captured on-site and in person (not downloaded from a website), list the city and institution. If the image was found in a book or serial, include the word *In* followed by the publication information of the work and the page number on which the image appears.

For original images produced in scholarly articles, magazines, or newspapers, it is sufficient to cite the work as a whole. See **APA Image Citations in the Reference List** for examples of how citations should appear in the reference list.

Example: APA Image Citations in the Reference List

Image Found on the Web
Nunley, D. (2012). *Big fish* [Photograph]. Retrieved from https://flic.kr/p/dHH6uu

Image from a Database
Motherwell, R. (1970). *Africa suite: Number 2* [Print]. Retrieved from *Artstor*.

Image from a Book
Cézanne, P. (1904–1906). *Mont Sainte-Victoire* [Oil painting]. In Sayre, H. M., *Writing about art* (6th ed.) (p. 53). Upper Saddle River, NJ: Pearson Prentice Hall, 2009.

Image from a Museum or Archive Website
Rembrandt Harmensz. van Rijn. (1642). *Militia Company of District II under the command of Captain Frans Banninck Cocq, Known as the 'Night Watch'* [Painting]. Retrieved from https://www.rijksmuseum.nl/nl/collectie/SK-C-5

Image in a Museum
Miró, J. (1980–1981). *Woman addressing the public: Project for a monument* [Sculpture]. Fort Worth, TX: Kimbell Art Museum.

Citing Images in MLA Style

In-Text Citations
When citing images in MLA style in the text of a paper, the creator's last name and the page number(s) from which the material came are included in parentheses after the cited material, like this: (Creator 54). If there is no creator, a title can be used instead: ("Title" 54). If there is no title, you should use whatever information comes first in the complete citation in the list of works cited. For

images found online, do not list a page number. Each in-text citation should clearly correspond to an item in the list of works cited.

Figures and Captions

In MLA style, images are called *figures,* and all images that are reproduced in a paper should be labeled as Fig. 1, Fig. 2, Fig. 3., and so on. Exceptions to this style are tables, which are labeled Table, and musical illustrations, which are labeled Ex. (for "Example").

Figures are placed as close to their reference in the text as possible. When referring to figures in the text, use lowercase letters, like this: (see fig. 1). Figure labels are placed below the figure, followed by a brief explanatory caption. If the figure caption contains complete citation information and is not referenced in the text, it is not necessary to include the item in the list of works cited.

MLA image captions follow this pattern:

Fig 1. Ann Author, *Title of Work,* Museum and/or Publication information. The following example shows how an image would be referenced in the text and caption.

Example: MLA Figure Reference in the Text

Painted toward the end of his life, El Greco's *The Adoration of the Shepherds* contains attenuated figures and striking contrasts between light and dark (see fig. 1).

Example: MLA Figure Caption

Fig. 1. El Greco (Domenikos Theotokopoulos), *The Adoration of the Shepherds,* The Metropolitan Museum of Art, Bequest of George Blumenthal, 1941 (41.190.17).

Works Cited List

Some variation exists in how images are cited in the MLA Works Cited list. However, MLA citations for images found online generally follow this pattern:

Creator, Creator. *Title of Material*. Year of Composition. Holding Entity. Title of Website or Database. Medium. Date of Access.

Figure 5.2 breaks down the different parts of an MLA entry for an image found online, as it would appear in the Works Cited list.

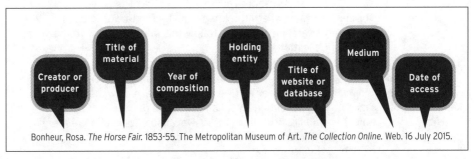

Bonheur, Rosa. *The Horse Fair*. 1853-55. The Metropolitan Museum of Art. *The Collection Online*. Web. 16 July 2015.

Figure 5.2. *Parts of an image citation in the MLA Works Cited list*

The **Elements of MLA Citations** chart describes these different elements in more detail for a variety of images types and sources.

Elements of MLA Citations

ELEMENT	CITATION FORMAT
Creator or producer	The creator's name is listed as Last name, First name. If no individual creator is listed, an organization may be used instead. For advertisements, begin with the name of the product or company. If no creator or organization is available, the citation begins with the title. When citing an image found online, use the proper name of the creator if available; however, if only a screen name is available, use that in the citation instead.
Title of image	Italicize the titles of works of art. If a map or chart appears to stand alone, italicize the title; if it appears to be part of a collection, place the title in quotation marks and include the title of the collection in italics. Place the titles of comic strips in quotation marks and place the source title in italics. If there is no title, as with a cartoon or advertisement, skip this part.
Year of composition	If no date is available, n.d. should be used instead. If necessary, a date range may be used (1990-1992) or a question mark can be used to indicate an uncertain date (1956?).

(continued)

ELEMENT	CITATION FORMAT
Medium of composition	When citing a work in its original context (i.e., Photograph, Map, Advertisement, Cartoon, or Comic strip), include the medium of composition. For reproductions of images online or in print, the medium of composition does not need to be included.
Other publication information	For works of visual art, list the institution that houses the work or the name of the private collection that the work is in, as well as the city where the institution or collection is located. For images found in books, follow this information with the publication information about the book, as well as the page, figure, or plate number where the image can be found. For images on museum or archive websites, follow this information with the online publication information.
Online publication information	MLA style does not require that a URL be included for images found online. Include the title of the database or website, the medium of publication (Web) and the date of access. If supplementary publication information is available for an image found online, that information can be included prior to listing the website or database name.

Example: MLA Image Citations in the Works Cited List

Image Found on the Web
Nunley, Donnie. *Big Fish.* 2012. *Flickr.* Web. 31 July 2014.

Image from a Database
Motherwell, Robert. *Africa Suite: Number 2.* 1970. *Artstor.* Web. 21 Aug. 2014.

Image from a Book
Cézanne, Paul. *Mont Sainte-Victoire.* 1904–6. *Writing about Art.* 6th ed. Henry M. Sayre.
    Upper Saddle River: Pearson Prentice Hall, 2009. 53. Print.

Image from a Museum
Miró, Joan. *Woman Addressing the Public: Project for a Monument.* 1980–81. Bronze.
    Kimbell Art Museum, Fort Worth.

CREDITING IMAGES

Crediting images with a credit statement is an alternative to a full academic citation and is an appropriate way to acknowledge authorship of an image in some circumstances. Credit statements give attribution to image creators, provide title and date information, and include a link to the original image. Credit statements are especially useful when writing for the Web. You can learn to use image credits in your own work, such as with images used to enliven research guides.

You can also teach these skills as part of any class where there is an assignment involving images with a web component such as a blog post or a website.

As with any citation practice, the first step in crediting images is to gather the relevant information about the image. Using images that give enough information to attribute them makes giving credit easier. **Activity 5.3: Crediting Images** takes students through the process of gathering information about an image and creating an image credit statement. At minimum, follow these tips:

- Give credit to the image creator.
- Provide a title and date (if available).
- Include the Creative Commons license type, if applicable.
- Link to the original work (page with the metadata).
- Follow any additional attribution instructions provided by the source.

Example: Sample Image Credits

General Format

Title by A. Creator, date (if available), via source (Creative Commons License Type, if applicable).

An aircraft view of high cirrus and stratocumulus undercast with altostratus, image ID wea00016 by the National Oceanic and Atmospheric Administration/Department of Commerce, via the NOAA Photo Library.

PROVIDING INFORMATION WITH IMAGES YOU CREATE

When creating and sharing images, it is important to provide information with the images so others can cite your work when they use or repost your image. Because we know how important it is to be able to find the basics about an image's creator, date, source information, and usage restrictions, it is clear that we all have a responsibility to provide such information with images we create and share. Adding a Creative Commons license or other rights statement can enhance the usability of your images, and your contribution to visual conversations will have greater impact.

Images you create may be entirely your own work, such as original photographs. You may also build on other people's images with collages or other creative adaptations. Image captions should reflect this adaptation and provide information about all contributions. Phrases such as "based on" or "including" can connect information about the new work with citation information about others' work that has been built upon or incorporated. The Creative Commons Wiki (wiki.creativecommons.org) includes best practices for attribution and illustrated examples for acknowledging material that you modified or used to create a derivative work.

Next Steps

Like all other resources, images must be cited. Once you feel comfortable with the whys of image citation, try some of the following:

- Practice gathering information needed to generate image citations.
- Credit images on any research guides, blogs, or websites that you write.
- Treat an image citation as a resource for further exploration.
- Provide textual information with images that you make available so that others can cite your work.

REFERENCES

American Psychological Association. 2010. *Publication Manual of the American Psychological Association.* Washington, DC: American Psychological Association.

Modern Language Association of America. 2009. *MLA Handbook for Writers of Research Papers.* New York, NY: Modern Language Association of America.

ACTIVITY 5.1

Why Cite Images?

LEARNING OUTCOMES

- Engage with questions about the purpose and function of citations.
- Relate citation to the scholarly communication process and participate in research as a conversation.

DESCRIPTION

Use the following discussion prompts to open a conversation about images and scholarly communication:

- How do scholars communicate with each other?
- What happens when scholars use images in their work?
- How do scholars communicate about image content?
- How do image citations facilitate that conversation?

VISUAL LITERACY STANDARDS CONNECTION

- ACRL Visual Literacy Standard 7, Performance Indicator 3

Gathering Information for Image Citations

LEARNING OUTCOMES

- Look carefully at text that accompanies images for context.
- Prepare for image citation.

DESCRIPTION

Students access an image related to the course or their research topics, in the image's original location or context, for the purpose of examining the information that accompanies it. Using an image they're familiar with or one that you provide, students complete the **Gathering Information for Image Citations Worksheet** and record the information they find about the image. Students can work in pairs or groups, helping each other gather the appropriate information. Conclude the exercise with a group discussion.

DISCUSSION PROMPTS

- Where did you look to find information about your image?
- What kinds of information did you discover?
- Was the text information different within different sources?
- Is there information you're lacking, and where might you go to find it?

TIP FOR SUCCESS

- Familiarize yourself with images related to the course, and work through the information-finding process with several of them. What challenges do you anticipate students will face as they try to find enough information for their citations?

OPTIONAL EXTENSIONS

- This activity can also be done as a class, examining image information together.
- Ask students to create a complete image citation using the information they have found.

VISUAL LITERACY STANDARDS CONNECTION

- ACRL Visual Literacy Standard 7, Performance Indicators 2 and 3

Gathering Information for Image Citations

Step 1: Bring up an image related to your research question or project.

Make sure you are looking at the image in its original context (wherever it originated or wherever you found it), such as its original website, museum website, article, blog, or other source.

Tip: If you found the image by using a web search engine such as Google Images, go to the image's original website to gather citation information.

Step 2: Within the image's original source, find out as much information as you can about the image and read any accompanying text.

Places you can find information about the image include the following:

- *Captions* accompanying the image
- *Tags* associated with the image
- *Text* on the same page as the image or surrounding the image
- *Reference pages* or bibliographies in an article
- The *website address* or URL

Step 3: Record information about your image.

Where did you find the image? Include the name of the website and the web address, the book citation and page number, the database name and image web address, or other source information.	
What is the title of the image? If there's no title, write down a brief description.	
Who made the image? This might be the photographer, artist, Flickr username, or the like.	
When was the image created? Find the most specific date you can.	
If the image is of a work of art or other object, *is it in a museum or archive?* Record the name and place here (for example, Seattle Art Museum, Seattle, Washington).	
Is *rights information* included with the image, such as a Creative Commons license or terms of use?	
Is there any other identifying information available about your image? Include it here.	
Is there information you'd like to know about your image for purposes of a citation but weren't able to find?	

Step 4: Compare notes and discuss your findings.

Crediting Images

LEARNING OUTCOME

- Give credit for images used in web-based communications and environments.

DESCRIPTION

Discuss the types of situations in which it is appropriate to use an image credit line, explaining how crediting images on web pages differs from citation in scholarly research papers. Review Creative Commons licenses and how to find Creative Commons images. Students find a Creative Commons image, then the **Crediting Images Worksheet** leads them through gathering information about the image and creating the image credit using the suggested format.

TIPS FOR SUCCESS

- Remind students that they need to do their best to give credit to the image creator, provide a title and date, link to the original work, and follow any attribution instructions and license information provided by the source.
- Prior to conducting this activity, review strategies for gathering information about images, especially those found on the Web.

VISUAL LITERACY STANDARDS CONNECTION

- ACRL Visual Literacy Standard 7, Performance Indicators 1, 2, and 3

Crediting Images

Find an image available under a Creative Commons license and complete the steps.

Step 1: Gather image information.

Provide the image title.
- The image is called: _____

Link to the original work.
- The image URL is: _____

Give credit to the image creator.
- The image was created by: _____

Include the image date.
- The date of the image is: _____

Make note of the image source.
- The source of the image is: _____

Follow attribution instructions provided by the source.

- The image creator asks me to: _____

- There is a Creative Commons license on this image, and it is: _____

Step 2: Create an image credit.

Example: Title by A. Creator, date, via source (CC License Type).

Following the preceding example, write your credit line here:

_____

_____

_____

_____

_____

Images and the Research Process

IMAGES CAN PROMPT inquiry and discovery and help students move from their concrete personal experiences into the more abstract area of library research. A deeper and richer understanding of visual content empowers students to think about ways to use images as part of their everyday iterative research processes. Teaching image research and evaluation alongside traditional bibliographic tools is a natural fit. If you're not sure where to begin, use the process and prompts in **Activity 6.1: Kick-Starting Research with Historical Images** to lead students through looking at the details of an image, describing cultural and historical factors relevant to the production of an image, and generating questions from an image.

Research shows that college students are already looking for images and text at the same time: in their information-seeking behavior, students don't separate searching for sources by type. In their 2010 Project Information Literacy report, Alison Head and Michael Eisenberg noted that "students begin their course-related research activities in search of *research contexts,* [which] entails getting information for interpreting and defining information need" (5–6). Head and Eisenberg went on to say that students often find this part of the research process to be "laborious" and "frustrating." Incorporating visual literacy as part of the research process can mitigate this frustration by giving students the tools to move through multiple sources and content types.

ACTIVITIES IN THIS CHAPTER

As they grapple with the richness of the contextual information they find, they build comfort with an information environment that blends image and text. Each source demands sharp evaluation skills to parse what's there and to pose new questions. Working with images throughout the research process readies students to find and use information in all formats, while developing critical thinking and evaluation proficiency.

Foundational Questions

What Do Images That I Encounter during Research Tell Me?

Pay attention to the variety and types of images that you find while you research—they can reveal disciplinary and interdisciplinary practices and serve as sources themselves. Images can raise new questions about your topic and give you more ideas for avenues to explore in your research.

Can Visual Thinking Techniques Help Me Understand My Topic and Research?

Take a moment to sketch out the concepts in your next research topic. Drawing a concept map, or using a graphic organizer, can further your research by revealing previously unseen connections, narratives, and arguments.

What Do the Visual Characteristics of My Sources Tell Me?

Evaluating the visual characteristics of sources can help you decode the purpose of a source and strengthen your critical reading and evaluation skills.

How Do I Approach Evaluating Images and Their Sources?

The critical thinking strategies you've developed for evaluating all kinds of information also work for evaluating images and image sources. Assess the unique characteristics of images and explore the reliability and credibility of where you find them to decide if an image aligns with your project goals.

Using Images to Further Research

Paying attention to the images that you encounter during the research process reveals disciplinary and interdisciplinary practices. These images can provide ideas for visual content to include in research or to use as sources of information themselves. Consider what you can learn from the range of images included in articles about the same topic, but in different fields. The **Images Found during Research** example parses the graphics retrieved by two searches in a multidisciplinary database—one for "solar panels" and one for "art therapy." As students are researching, directing their attention to the images included in the sources they find can advance their understanding of how images are used in scholarly discourse. Indeed, many subscription databases emphasize image content as value added and include features that let you delve into the graphics without even reading the article. Contemplating the variation in graphic choices across the disciplines opens up discussion with students about discourse communities, helping students make choices about graphics to include in their own projects as they move from novices to experts. Chapter 3, "Create and Use Images," applies this concept in the image creation process; use **Activity 3.1: Exploring Disciplinary Image Use** to help students move from pinpointing image use in a discipline to applying what they learn in their own work.

Example: Images Found during Research

Search 1: "Solar Panels"

SAMPLE ARTICLE	INCLUDED GRAPHICS	DISCIPLINE
Aly, Aly Mousaad, and Girma Bitsuamlak. 2014. "Wind-Induced Pressures on Solar Panels Mounted on Residential Homes." *Journal of Architectural Engineering* 20 (1): 1–12.	2 Color Photographs 2 Charts 12 Graphs	Engineering
Smith, Michael G., and Johannes Urpelainen. 2014. "Early Adopters of Solar Panels in Developing Countries: Evidence from Tanzania." *Review of Policy Research* 31 (1): 17–37.	8 Charts	Public Policy
Zhang Yinong, Pu Jiantao, and Jianjun Fang. 2014. "Machine Vision Based Micro-Crack Inspection in Thin-Film Solar Cell Panel." *Sensors and Transducers* 179 (9): 157–161.	2 Black-and-White Photographs 1 Diagram 1 Graph	Applied Technology

Search 2: "Art Therapy"

SAMPLE ARTICLE	INCLUDED GRAPHICS	DISCIPLINE
Crawford, Cindy, Courtney Lee, and John Bingham. 2014. "Sensory Art Therapies for the Self-Management of Chronic Pain Symptoms." *Pain Medicine* 15 (S1): S66-S75.	2 Diagrams 4 Charts	Medicine
Metzl, Einat S. 2013. "Artistic, Therapeutic, and Sexually Informed: A Five-Week Human Sexuality Course for Art Therapy Students." *American Journal of Sexuality Education* 8 (4): 191-212.	3 Illustrations 1 Collage 1 Photograph 7 Graphs	Education
Holmqvist, Gärd, and Cristina Lundqvist Persson. 2012. "Is There Evidence for the Use of Art Therapy in Treatment of Psychosomatic Disorders, Eating Disorders and Crisis? A Comparative Study of Two Different Systems for Evaluation." *Scandinavian Journal of Psychology* 53 (1): 47-53.	1 Diagram 3 Charts	Psychology

Wherever they are used, images can act as a springboard for further research. Images contain a wealth of information and are a rich source for digging deeper into your content and research area. Images encountered during research typically are not there simply for decorative purposes. Consider what an image is adding to an argument and how you can follow that argument to ask more questions and explore other sources. In **Activity 6.2: Using Images to Further Research,** students assemble images they encounter during a research session, then use these images to pose new questions and move the research process forward.

Visualizing a Topic

Flex visual literacy skills at the beginning of the research process by engaging students in visualizing their topics. You may be accustomed to asking students to brainstorm keywords for a research topic. Instead of listing keywords, why not have students generate a concept map by drawing a circle in the center of a page and creating branches for subtopics and related ideas. Or give students a few minutes at the beginning of a workshop to draw an "ideal source," then use the results as a springboard to decide which resources to consult. Representing research ideas in a nonlinear way encourages lateral thinking and can reveal new connections.

Figure 6.1. *Brainstorming*

Visualizing a topic also shows promise for developing and improving higher order thinking. A study in *Education* found that students who made concept maps about a psychology-related topic later demonstrated superior critical thinking about that topic. The study concluded that "graphically depicting the structure of complex concepts appears to effectively complement the variety of abstract paradigms for facilitating critical thinking" (Harris and Zha 2013, 209). There is an abundance of research in medical, pharmaceutical, and nursing education about using concept maps in the classroom. One such study, conducted by a team of pharmacy educators at the University of the Pacific, found that the majority of students enrolled in a cardiovascular care course agreed that concept maps helped them to conceptualize the big picture of treatment for the chronic conditions studied in the course (Carr-Lopez et al. 2014).

Evaluating Visual Characteristics of Sources

Librarians often help students distinguish between scholarly and popular articles, unpacking textual cues to uncover authority, accuracy, purpose, quality, objectivity, currency, and relevance. By extension, we can help students identify how the visual characteristics of a source contribute to the interpretation of its overall reliability and usefulness. Instead of starting with the written

☕ **COFFEE BREAK!**

Concept Mapping

In the box, sketch a concept map for a topic you've recently worked with students to explore.

REFLECT

What new connections did you find?

How might students benefit from this strategy?

criteria, try a side-by-side visual comparison to prompt discussion. Have students explain the differences that they *see*. For example, students can compare

- A recent cover of the journal *Popular Music* with a recent cover of *Rolling Stone*
- A feature article from *Science* with an article from *National Geographic*

This type of work trains our students to use visual cues to compare and contrast layout, ads, images, titles, headings, and authorship. This approach is transferable and sets up students to ask critical questions of sources that they encounter in different contexts, such as a list of database search results or a website that relates to a research topic. For example, a student might notice that a website's red, white, and blue color scheme suggests a strong patriotic stance or that the images of people in a political candidate's blog all look directly at the camera, portraying a feeling of strength. The use of big, bold headlines on a newspaper's site reveals the content creator's desire to draw viewers in and perhaps persuade them about a particular point of view. Use **Activity 6.3: Examining a Source Visually** to examine how bibliographic information is presented, to explore design elements, and to consider how visual elements inform a source's authority, purpose, objectivity, and reliability.

 COFFEE BREAK!

Explore the Geography of a Source

Pick up a book, magazine, or journal. Take a moment to step back and look at it visually. Try to find each piece of bibliographic information, and classify your efforts in the table using the following scale to determine each item's visual emphasis score:

1 = Impossible to find
2 = Difficult to find
3 = Not easy to find, but I found it
4 = Easy to find
5 = Impossible to miss

INFORMATION	VISUAL EMPHASIS SCORE (1-5)	NOTES AND QUESTIONS
Title		
Author(s)		
Author(s)' affiliation		
Publisher		
Date of publication		
Sources used		

Which pieces of information stand out? Which are difficult to find? What new questions arise?

REFLECT

How might you apply this exercise in your work with students?

Evaluating Images and Their Sources

Evaluating images is an extension of the information evaluation you're already doing with text-based materials. Critical thinking, contextualizing, and inquiry practices are the foundation of all evaluation, including image and image source evaluation. The nature of the image format, however, requires that you expand your evaluation strategies to encompass additional image-specific questions and questions raised by the relationship of text and image.

We like to think of image evaluation in clusters of questions or sites of evaluation. Some clusters are already part of your everyday information evaluation practice. Other clusters may prompt new ideas to help you and your students evaluate image content quickly and effectively. Different clusters may be more relevant at different times, but having these tools at your fingertips can make it that much easier to seamlessly integrate image and image source evaluation into the research process. Use **Activity 6.4: Evaluating Images and Their Sources** to think through the different aspects of image evaluation with your students, faculty, and colleagues.

EVALUATING IMAGES RHETORICALLY

The context in which an image will be used is key to the evaluation process. Compositionist Joseph Bizup introduced a rhetorical vocabulary for teaching research-based writing dubbed BEAM, for background, exhibit, argument, and method (Bizup 2008). With BEAM, students focus on *how* a source is used

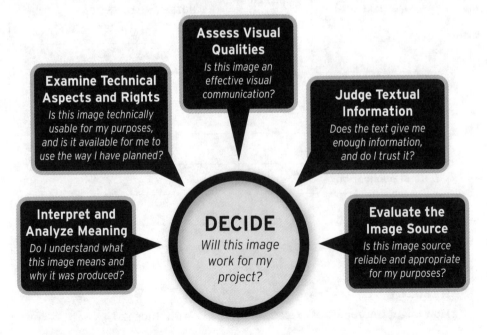

Figure 6.2. *Image evaluation clusters*

rather than on the source type or classification. Bizup argues that classifying sources as primary, secondary, or tertiary ignores their rhetorical function in favor of their "relationship to some external point of reference."

Classic definitions of primary sources (created during the time period or culture under study), secondary sources (discuss primary sources), and tertiary sources (summarize secondary sources) can undermine a more complex rhetorical understanding of what role a source is playing within a work. The BEAM model complements a basic understanding of the characteristics of source types while offering the flexibility to see that ways of using sources are context-dependent and shift based on discipline and research question.

Like writing instructors, librarians can use a source's rhetorical role to develop critical thinking and move beyond prescriptive evaluative criteria such as the "CRAAP Test," which emphasizes currency, relevance, authority, accuracy, and purpose but fails to address the role that sources play in a student's work. Although BEAM focuses on textual sources, it can be applied to visual materials too. Our chart **Evaluate an Image's Rhetorical Role** shows how images can be background, exhibit, argument, and method sources. It is important to remember that because BEAM is context-based, a specific source may fit into different categories, depending on how the author intends to use it.

Evaluate an Image's Rhetorical Role

SOURCE	RHETORICAL ROLE	IMAGE EXAMPLE
Background	Provides general information, factual evidence, or context; often encyclopedias or reference materials	A statistical chart to track historical unemployment rates
Exhibit	Analyzes or interprets; often primary source materials such as documents, ephemera, or data	A soup-can label with recipes from the 1950s to interpret elements of social life from that time period
Argument	Engages in scholarly conversation by refuting, affirming, or refining claims; often journal articles or scholarly papers	An exhibit catalog of Salvador Dali's work to make an argument about surrealism
Method	Derives governing concept or way of working; often theory sources	A diagram of a theoretical model to ground new work

Bizup proposes a simple rule of thumb to help writers avoid creating stale prose when contributing new ideas to scholarly discourse: "If you start with an exhibit, look for argument sources to engage; if you start with argument sources, look for exhibits to interpret" (Bizup 2008, 82). Exhibits are often primary sources, and you can deploy this rule of thumb to identify when students might need a primary source to push their work forward.

Images and Information Literacy Threshold Concepts

We have already taken an in-depth look at what visual literacy looks like up close and in daily practice. In this section, we take a broader view and situate images and visual literacy within the context of ACRL's *Framework for Information Literacy for Higher Education*. Images fit into every aspect of information literacy, from reflectively discovering information to understanding how information is produced and valued to using information to create new knowledge and participate ethically in communities of learning.

The *Framework*'s six frames—each consisting of a threshold concept, knowledge practices, and dispositions—offer a flexible structure that can be used in tandem with visual literacy competencies to enhance library instruction and student learning across the disciplines. Threshold concepts open up new possibilities for visual literacy engagement, and visual literacy practices can expand that liminal space where librarians and students are exploring complex ideas such as the value of information and the information creation process. Visual literacy can enrich, deepen, and make tangible students' experience of information literacy. Our real-world classroom examples for each frame provide a taste of what's possible.

AUTHORITY IS CONSTRUCTED AND CONTEXTUAL

Like other information sources, images and graphics reflect their creators' expertise and credibility and must be evaluated on the communication purpose *and* the context in which they are situated. The information need and purpose determine the level of authority required. For example, if you need an image of an air conditioner part so that you can buy a new one from your local hardware store, a photo you take of the broken part might be just fine. But a student who is planning to use a 3-D printer to generate a new part on her own will need a more sophisticated visual model.

Maps work well for teaching this frame because students tend to automatically view them as authoritative sources. In **Activity 6.5: Analyzing a Map**

to Teach Source Evaluation, students answer a series of questions to judge the credibility of a map as a source for making a prediction. Students learn that maps are authored constructions of three-dimensional reality, prone to distortions, biases, artistic license, creative embellishment, and even lies.

INFORMATION CREATION AS A PROCESS

Whether they stand alone or are integrated into academic work, images are created for specific purposes to communicate messages, convey ideas, or illustrate concepts. Chapter 3, "Create and Use Images," provides a range of activities that work toward building a sophisticated understanding of the image creation process. Reinforce this frame by incorporating image evaluation into conversations about the research process. Use our **Evaluating Images and Their Sources Worksheet** to help students articulate the capabilities and constraints of visual content created through any medium or process.

INFORMATION HAS VALUE

The economics of image production and distribution is a rich area for discussing concepts related to this frame. Use **Activity 6.6: Contemplating the Value of an Image** to explore some of the choices that photographers and corporations make when sharing and selling images. The case study in this activity illustrates how the "value" of an image can range from economic to communal, reflecting a variety of interests and motivations. Chapter 4, "Ethical Use of Images," explores intellectual property principles and practices around images, such as fair use, interpreting terms of use, censorship, and ethical issues related to image sharing.

RESEARCH AS INQUIRY

Use images to emphasize the iterative nature of research and to guide students through the process of generating new questions or refining existing questions. In **Activity 6.2: Using Images to Further Research**, students collect images during the research process and then spend time analyzing the images to raise new questions that push their research forward. Used in this way, images help students to develop a curious mind-set and the flexible thought processes needed to articulate knowledge gaps and determine next steps in the research process. Chapter 1, "Interpret and Analyze Images," provides key questions for inquiry-based learning with a variety of image content, ranging from photographs to data visualizations.

SCHOLARSHIP AS CONVERSATION

Images can hook audience members, capture their interest, and add cohesion to a research workshop. The analogy of scholarship as a conversation is a perfect occasion for using an image as a topic of conversation. We've all had conversations, and we know what they look like and where they happen. Consider beginning a research workshop with an iconic image or an image commonly known in the subject area. Then ask students to imagine that they are in a space such as a café or lounge and that it is full of people deeply engaged in conversation about the image—the students' task is to engage in one of the conversations going on around them. Give students a minute to write down what they would do to join one of the conversations. Students might say, "I'd need to introduce myself" or "I'd have to think of something to say about the image." And inevitably someone says, "I'd have to *listen*" or "I'd have to ask someone else more about the image first." These answers set the tone for the session and let you draw on the analogy of research as a conversation throughout the class. **Activity 5.1: Why Cite Images?** situates images in the scholarly communication process by relating image citation practices to participating in research as a conversation.

SEARCHING AS STRATEGIC EXPLORATION

Unlike textual sources, most images lack full bibliographic descriptions. This difference means that searching for images requires a healthy dose of creativity and flexible thinking. For example, to effectively use a corpus of images described only by user-generated tags, a student needs to imagine an ideal image, think about how someone else might describe it, try a search, and then modify that search based on the results. Or a student might need to accept that using the browsing functionality in an image database is the best bet. Exploring image sources can help students tolerate ambiguity and build a skill set of strategies that transfer to finding other types of information. In chapter 2, "Find the Right Images," we provide detailed strategies for image inquiry and discovery.

Next Steps

Images are part of, or can be integrated into, every step of the research process. Incorporate images into your own work whenever possible.

- Take a moment to visually evaluate the next source you use.
- Try incorporating the BEAM model into your teaching of image source types.
- Next time you're discussing information literacy threshold concepts with your colleagues, make images a part of the conversation.

COFFEE BREAK!

Create a Visual Prompt for Scholarship as Conversation

Compositionists use literary theorist Kenneth Burke's analogy of scholarly discourse as an unending conversation, often called "the Burkean parlor," to teach writing. The research process involves "listening in" on this "unending conversation," and you can use an image as a visual prompt to convey this analogy.

Read the following excerpt and then brainstorm a visual.

> Imagine that you enter a parlor. You come late. When you arrive, others have long preceded you, and they are engaged in a heated discussion, a discussion too heated for them to pause and tell you exactly what it is about. In fact, the discussion had already begun long before any of them got there, so that no one present is qualified to retrace for you all the steps that had gone before. You listen for a while, until you decide that you have caught the tenor of the argument; then you put in your oar. Someone answers; you answer him; another comes to your defense; another aligns himself against you, to either the embarrassment or gratification of your opponent, depending upon the quality of your ally's assistance. However, the discussion is interminable. The hour grows late, you must depart. And you do depart, with the discussion still vigorously in progress. (Burke 1941, 110)

List conversation spaces that might resonate with your learners (e.g., campus lounges, nearby cafés, or actual parlors).

_____   _____

_____   _____

_____   _____

Select a space and use an image of it to create a visual prompt.

Use your prompt as a warm-up to begin a research workshop. Students draw on their prior experiences as they consider this question: "What would you do to join in on a conversation in this space?" Use the responses as a touchstone for the "scholarship as a conversation" frame.

REFLECT

What did you learn from the students' responses?

REFERENCES

Bizup, Joseph. 2008. "BEAM: A Rhetorical Vocabulary for Teaching Research-Based Writing." *Rhetoric Review* 27 (1): 72–86.

Burke, Kenneth. 1941. *The Philosophy of Literary Form Studies in Symbolic Action.* Baton Rouge: Louisiana State University.

Carr-Lopez, Sian M., Suzanne M. Galal, Deepti Vyas, Rajul A. Patel, and Eric H. Gnesa. 2014. "The Utility of Concept Maps to Facilitate Higher-Level Learning in a Large Classroom Setting." *American Journal of Pharmaceutical Education* 78 (9): 1–7.

Harris, Charles M., and Shenghua Zha. 2013. "Concept Mapping: A Critical Thinking Technique." *Education* 134 (2): 207–211.

Head, Alison J., and Michael B. Eisenberg. 2010. "Truth Be Told: How College Students Evaluate and Use Information in the Digital Age." *SSRN.* dx.doi .org/10.2139/ssrn.2281485.

Kick-Starting Research with Historical Images

LEARNING OUTCOMES

- Look carefully at the details of an image.
- Describe cultural and historical factors relevant to the production of an image.
- Generate questions from an image.

DESCRIPTION

The activity is laid out in two parts: an individual reflection on an image, followed by a class discussion about what can be learned from exploring the image's context. Prepare a two-slide presentation: slide one contains only the image, and slide two includes the image source, title, and any relevant accompanying metadata. Show slide one while students respond to questions on the worksheet. Questions move along the continuum of critical inquiry by first sharpening observational skills and eventually requiring students to articulate what new questions the image raises. After discussing responses to the questions, reveal slide two with the image information.

For example, if slide one is figure 6.3, slide two would contain the following:

- From the Library of Congress American Memory Project.
- Titled "Bread line beside the Brooklyn Bridge Approach."
- Created during the Great Depression as part of the Farm Security Administration's effort to record American life between 1935 and 1944.
- Part of the same series as Dorothea Lange's iconic image of the Depression, "Migrant Mother," formally titled "Destitute pea pickers in California. Mother of seven children. Age thirty-two. Nipomo, California."

TIPS FOR SUCCESS

- For maximum impact, choose a high-quality image that is closely related to the course content and was created at a known time for a specific purpose. Photographs created as part of a government project or for a journalistic purpose work especially well.
- This activity is an excellent opener to a one-shot session because it grabs students' attention and immediately engages them in the looking process. The success of this activity hinges on your ability to lead a purposeful and directed discussion, so choose the image carefully.

OPTIONAL EXTENSIONS

- Present the image and accompanying metadata at the same time. Students individually generate a list of questions, then work in groups to compare and contrast their work and generate a new list of questions. Discuss findings as a class.
- Analyze an image's suggestive qualities, aesthetic elements, or relation to ideas or concepts. Present an image, then use the following discussion prompts:

  ◊ What mood, atmosphere, or emotional quality does the image evoke? What do you feel while looking at it?
  ◊ How do the aesthetic elements of the image contribute to this feeling, atmosphere, or quality? Consider the use of color, line, shape, texture, and light and dark.
  ◊ What idea or concept might this image be used to represent? Why?

VISUAL LITERACY STANDARDS CONNECTION

- ACRL Visual Literacy Standard 3, Performance Indicators 1, 2, and 4

Figure 6.3. *New York, New York. Bread line beside the Brooklyn Bridge Approach, via the Library of Congress, Prints and Photographs Division, FSA/OWI Collection (LC-USW33–035391-ZC)*

Kick-Starting Research with Historical Images

Step 1: Analyze the image on your own.

Explore the image and respond to the following questions:

- What do I see? _____
_____

- What is going on? _____
_____
_____

- Why do I think this image was created? _____
_____
_____

Step 2: Investigate the image as a group.

Take your initial observations further and record your thoughts here:

- What do you see that gives you a sense of the time period in which this image was created?
_____
_____

- What do you see that indicates where this image was created? _____
_____
_____

- Does this image clue you in on economic conditions? Political conditions? Social structures?
How? _____
_____
_____

- What questions does this image raise for you? _____
_____
_____

Using Images to Further Research

LEARNING OUTCOMES

- Retrieve and collect images during the research process.
- Analyze images to raise new questions for research.

DESCRIPTION

Use a tool such as Padlet during a research session for students to capture, collect, and share images they find that relate to their topics. Padlet is a free virtual bulletin board that allows for sharing images and text. As students research their topics, have them drop images they encounter into a shared Padlet that you set up ahead of time. Images can be anything, and students do not need to interpret or evaluate the images during the initial phase of research. The Padlet acts as a holding tank for images, a brainstorming location for collecting visual materials. At the end of the research session, have students return to the images in the Padlet and consider the discussion questions individually or in small groups. Use the discussion prompts to find out how students will use the images they found to further their research.

DISCUSSION PROMPTS

- What new questions do these images raise about your research topic?
- What else do you need to explore, based on what you see?
- What other images do you still need to find?

TIPS FOR SUCCESS

- Set up the Padlet in advance, and make sure students retain access so they can return to the images and explore further after the class.
- Padlet is an ideal tool for this activity because student logins are not required, links to the original source are retained, and there's no need to download and track the image information.

VISUAL LITERACY STANDARDS CONNECTION

- ACRL Visual Literacy Standard 2, Performance Indicator 2
- ACRL Visual Literacy Standard 3, Performance Indicator 1

Examining a Source Visually

LEARNING OUTCOMES

- Examine visual characteristics of a source.
- Evaluate how information is presented visually.

DESCRIPTION

Select a source for students to evaluate visually, or have students select their own. Students work in groups to describe how elements such as title, author, and publisher are presented visually, recording their impressions on the **Examining a Source Visually Worksheet**. Prompt students to consider a variety of design elements and strategies, including layout, color, font, and emphasis. Then prompt students to reflect on what their descriptions reveal about the source's authority, purpose, objectivity, and reliability.

DISCUSSION PROMPTS

- What conclusions did you draw about the source based on its design?
- Does your analysis of the source tell you anything about how design choices are used when a content creator wants to persuade the reader to adopt a specific opinion or call to action?
- How are design choices used when a content creator wants to convey an objective stance?
- Based on your visual analysis, how would you evaluate the source's authority, purpose, and reliability?

TIP FOR SUCCESS

- This activity works well with any assignment that requires source evaluation, and it works particularly well when students have a research project that requires them to convey information visually.

OPTIONAL EXTENSIONS

- Try this activity exclusively with a specific source type, such as websites.
- If you are providing sources to students, also provide a text-only version of the source, stripped of all visual design. Consider giving half the class the original source and half the class the text-only version. How do students' evaluations of the source change or compare?

VISUAL LITERACY STANDARDS CONNECTION

- ACRL Visual Literacy Standard 3, Performance Indicator 3
- ACRL Visual Literacy Standard 4, Performance Indicator 2

Examining a Source Visually

Complete the following steps for your source.

Step 1: Explore the geography of the source.

Describe the visual presentation of the main pieces of identifying information. Where do they appear on the page? How are color, type, font size, and other visual cues used to draw your eye toward or away from particular information?

INFORMATION	DESCRIPTION OF VISUAL PRESENTATION
Title	
Author(s)	
Author(s)' affiliation	
Publisher	
Date	
Main content	
Other elements	

Step 2: Reflect.

How do the visual characteristics of the source impact the message that is being conveyed?

_____

_____

_____

How would you evaluate the source's authority, purpose, and reliability based on your descriptions?

_____

_____

_____

_____

Evaluating Images and Their Sources

LEARNING OUTCOME

- Evaluate images and their sources from a variety of perspectives.

DESCRIPTION

The **Evaluating Images and Their Sources Worksheet** provides a question-driven approach to evaluating images and image sources. The question clusters are nonhierarchical, so students respond to the ones that apply to their specific context. These questions can be used in consultations with faculty and students, in library instruction sessions, in professional development workshops, and by faculty across the disciplines.

TIP FOR SUCCESS

- When working with these questions, emphasize that some questions may be more applicable than others, depending on the circumstances and the researcher's overall goals.

OPTIONAL EXTENSION

- Create an image evaluation workshop by presenting groups of students with the title and description of each question cluster. Give students time to generate their own criteria. Then give students the worksheet and discuss the overlaps and diversions.

VISUAL LITERACY STANDARDS CONNECTION

- ACRL Visual Literacy Standard 4, Performance Indicator 1, 2, 3, and 4

Evaluating Images and Their Sources

Use the clusters of questions to evaluate images and their sources and then decide if an image is right for your project. Some questions may be more applicable than others, so use the clusters that most suit your purposes.

❶ Interpret and Analyze Meaning

Do I understand what this image means and why it was produced?

☐ Have I worked through the process of interpreting this image?

☐ Would it be useful for me to investigate this image further?

❷ Examine Technical Aspects and Rights

Is this image technically usable for my purposes, and is it available for me to use the way I have planned?

☐ Is this image large enough and in a format I can use?

☐ Is the image clear and sharp enough?

☐ What do I know about how this image was produced?

☐ Has the image been altered in a way that calls into question its reliability?

☐ Does the rights information allow me to use this image the way I want to?

❸ Assess Visual Qualities

Is this image an effective visual communication?

☐ Is the intended message of this image aligned with how it is presented visually?

☐ Do color, design, and composition enhance or detract from the image's purpose?

☐ Is the information in the image consistent or at odds with information from other sources?

❹ Judge Textual Information

Does the text give me enough information, and do I trust it?

☐ Is the image accompanied by enough metadata and textual information that I can identify the image and investigate it further?

☐ Is the textual information consistent with what I see in the image, or does it raise further questions I need to resolve?

☐ Who provided the textual information, and what are their qualifications to do so?

☐ If the image is a data visualization, is the source of the data clear and are the variables clearly labeled?

❺ Evaluate the Image Source

Is this image source reliable and appropriate for my purposes?

☐ What do I know about this image source?

☐ Who maintains the source?

☐ Where does the source get the images it is making available?

☐ Does this source credit other sources for images it does not own or produce?

☐ Is the meaning of the image changed or manipulated by the context in which it appears?

☐ Is this the best source for the image, or should I keep exploring other sources?

Decide

Will this image work for my project, or not?

☐ Is this image relevant to my research or project?

☐ Is this image suitable for the purpose I have in mind?

☐ Do I want to save this image and its information for later use?

Analyzing a Map to Teach Source Evaluation

LEARNING OUTCOMES
- Interpret and analyze the meaning of a map.
- Judge the credibility of a map as a source of information.

DESCRIPTION

This activity is designed as a visual prompt for the evaluation of sources. It is arranged in two parts that correspond to steps 1 and 2 of the **Analyzing a Map Worksheet**. First, students look at a map and interpret and analyze its meaning. Then students identify the author and publisher, data sources, and methodology to determine whether the map is a credible source. After each step, use the think-pair-share technique, with pen and paper or polling software, to record individual observations and discuss in groups and as a class.

For example, if the topic is whether the Fukushima nuclear disaster could happen in the United States, you might use the following maps:

- Global Earthquake Activity Since 1973 and Nuclear Power Plant Locations by James, maptd, a blog about maps.
- Nuclear Power Plants and Earthquake Risk by the National Center for Disaster Preparedness, Earth Institute and Columbia University.

TIPS FOR SUCCESS
- This activity gives students practice in observing, interpreting, and judging the value of graphical information. Use a good or bad example or both together to compare and contrast.
- Select a map with different levels of credibility—for example, the data sources might be reliable, but the authorship or methods used to create the map are questionable. Initially students may automatically trust a map until they begin to dig deeper and ask more questions.

OPTIONAL EXTENSION
- This activity also can be used to demonstrate how research is a question-driven process. Ask students to analyze the rhetorical situation of the map (purpose, audience, message, creator), the validity of the map's claims (argument), and how the map can be used as a launching point (exhibit) to generate compelling research questions. Ask questions such as these: What else do you want to know? What is missing?

VISUAL LITERACY STANDARDS CONNECTION
- ACRL Visual Literacy Standard 3, Performance Indicator 1
- ACRL Visual Literacy Standard 4, Performance Indicator 1

With contribution from Russ White.

Analyzing a Map

Look at the map and answer the following questions.

Step 1: Observe and interpret.

1. What is the map presenting? _____

_____

2. Consider the following:
   What are the components (variables)? _____

_____

What do the colors represent? _____

_____

_____

Why do you think this map was created (for what purpose)? _____

_____

Step 2: Evaluate.

3. Who created the map? _____

_____

4. What are the sources of data and methods used to create the map? _____

_____

_____

5. Do you trust this map? Why or why not? _____

_____

_____

6. Would you use this map as evidence to support your argument in a research assignment?
   Why or why not? _____

_____

_____

Contemplating the Value of an Image

LEARNING OUTCOMES
- Consider different perspectives on the value of an image.
- Discuss real-world implications of Creative Commons licenses.

DESCRIPTION

Students explore the case of a commercial entity selling posters of photographer Frank Schulenburg's "The Bridge" by reading and discussing different perspectives on Creative Commons–licensed works. Have students form two large groups. Group 1 reads a newspaper article about this issue while group 2 reads a blog post by Frank Schulenburg. Students complete the **Contemplating the Value of an Image Worksheet** and then educate one another about the different perspectives during discussion.

READINGS
- *Group 1*: Douglas MacMillan, "Fight Over Yahoo's Use of Flickr Photos," *Wall Street Journal*, November 24, 2014.
- *Group 2*: Frank Schulenburg, "Why Yahoo Selling Canvas Prints from My Free Images Uploaded to Flickr Doesn't Bother Me," *Frank Schulenburg Landscape, Travel & Wikipedia Photography* (blog), November 30, 2014.

DISCUSSION PROMPTS
- What are the different kinds of value people place on photography?
- How would you feel if you were in the position of the photographer?
- Which Creative Commons license would you choose for your photography?

TIP FOR SUCCESS
- A bit of background knowledge helps this activity go smoothly. Frank Schulenburg shares many of his photos on Flickr with a CC BY-SA license, including his photograph titled "The Bridge." In 2014, Yahoo, the owner of Flickr, began selling posters of this image. Schulenburg was not notified, nor did he receive compensation. The situation created controversy in the media. However, Schulenburg felt that this was an acceptable and desired outcome—he values sharing content and even anticipated that his work could be used for profit.

OPTIONAL EXTENSIONS
- Expand the activity by having students read the news article and the blog post, then have them choose a side.
- Pair this activity with an in-depth exploration of Creative Commons licenses. Ask students to review the CC BY-SA license and determine whether it was followed in the instances described.

VISUAL LITERACY STANDARDS CONNECTION
- ACRL Visual Literacy Standard 7, Performance Indicator 1

Contemplating the Value of an Image

Step 1: Read the article that corresponds to your group.

Group 1

Douglas MacMillan, "Fight Over Yahoo's Use of Flickr Photos," *Wall Street Journal*, November 24, 2014, www.wsj.com/articles/fight-over-flickrs-use-of-photos-1416875564.

Group 2

Frank Schulenburg, "Why Yahoo Selling Canvas Prints from My Free Images Uploaded to Flickr Doesn't Bother Me," *Frank Schulenburg Landscape, Travel & Wikipedia Photography* (blog), November 30, 2014, www.wikiphotographer.net/why-yahoo-selling-canvas-prints-from -my-free-images-uploaded-to-flickr-doesnt-bother-me.

Step 2: Answer the following questions and be prepared to discuss your responses.

1. How would you describe the value placed on photography presented by this article?

_____

_____

_____

_____

2. How would you feel if you were in the position of the photographer in this reading?

_____

_____

_____

_____

3. Would you consider assigning a Creative Commons license to your own photography?

_____

_____

_____

_____

APPENDIX

ACRL Visual Literacy Competency Standards for Higher Education

Standards, Performance Indicators, and Learning Outcomes

Standard One

The visually literate student determines the nature and extent of the visual materials needed.

PERFORMANCE INDICATORS

1. ***The visually literate student defines and articulates the need for an image.***

   Learning Outcomes
   a. Defines the purpose of the image within the project (e.g., illustration, evidence, primary source, focus of analysis, critique, commentary)
   b. Defines the scope (e.g., reach, audience) and environment (e.g., academic environment, open web) of the planned image use
   c. Articulates criteria that need to be met by the image (e.g., subject, pictorial content, color, resolution, specific item)
   d. Identifies key concepts and terms that describe the needed image
   e. Identifies discipline-specific conventions for image use

2. ***The visually literate student identifies a variety of image sources, materials, and types.***

   Learning Outcomes
   a. Explores image sources to increase familiarity with available images and generate ideas for relevant image content

b. Investigates the scope, content, and potential usefulness of a range of image sources and formats (e.g., digital, print, subscription databases, open web, books or articles, repositories, personal creations)

c. Identifies different image and visual media types and materials (e.g., paintings, prints, photographs, born-digital images, data models)

d. Articulates ways images can be used to communicate data and information (e.g., charts, graphs, maps, diagrams, models, renderings, elevations)

e. Recognizes that existing images can be modified or repurposed to produce new visual content

---

Standard Two

The visually literate student finds and accesses needed images and visual media effectively and efficiently.

PERFORMANCE INDICATORS

1. *The visually literate student selects the most appropriate sources and retrieval systems for finding and accessing needed images and visual media.*

   Learning Outcomes

   a. Identifies interdisciplinary and discipline-specific image sources

   b. Articulates the advantages and disadvantages of various types of image sources and retrieval systems

   c. Recognizes how the image search process is affected by image rights and use restrictions

   d. Uses specialized online or in-person services to select image sources (e.g., online research guides, image and reference librarians, curators, archivists, disciplinary experts)

   e. Selects the most appropriate image sources for the current project

2. *The visually literate student conducts effective image searches.*

   Learning Outcomes

   a. Develops a search strategy appropriate to the image need and aligned with available resources

   b. Recognizes the role of textual information in providing access to image content, and identifies types of textual information and metadata typically associated with images (e.g., captions or other descriptions, personal or user-generated tags, creator information, repository names, title keywords, descriptions of visual content)

   c. Recognizes that images are often organized differently than text-based information and that this affects the way images can be accessed (e.g., absence of full-text search, variations in controlled vocabularies, lack of subject terms)

   d. Identifies keywords, synonyms, and related terms for the image needed, and maps those terms to the vocabulary used in the image source

   e. Uses images to find other images through exploration, social linking, visual search engines, or browsing

   f. Performs image and topical research concurrently, with each informing the other in an iterative resource-gathering process

g. Assesses the quality, quantity, and appropriateness of images retrieved, and revises the search strategy as necessary

3. *The visually literate student acquires and organizes images and source information.*

Learning Outcomes

a. Retrieves or reproduces the needed image using appropriate technologies or systems (e.g., download functions, copy and paste, scanning, cameras)
b. Accesses physical objects as needed to support the image research objective (e.g., site visits to archives, repositories, museums, galleries, libraries)
c. Organizes images and the information that accompanies them for personal retrieval, reuse, and scholarly citation

Standard Three

The visually literate student interprets and analyzes the meanings of images and visual media.

PERFORMANCE INDICATORS

1. *The visually literate student identifies information relevant to an image's meaning.*

Learning Outcomes

a. Looks carefully at an image and observes content and physical details
b. Reads captions, metadata, and accompanying text to learn about an image
c. Identifies the subject of an image
d. Examines the relationships of images to each other and uses related images to inform interpretation
e. Recognizes when more information about an image is needed, develops questions for further research, and conducts additional research as appropriate

2. *The visually literate student situates an image in its cultural, social, and historical contexts.*

Learning Outcomes

a. Describes cultural and historical factors relevant to the production of an image (e.g., time period, geography, economic conditions, political structures, social practices)
b. Examines the purposes and meanings of an image in its original context
c. Explores choices made in the production of an image to construct meaning or influence interpretation (e.g., framing, composition, included or excluded elements, staging)
d. Describes the intended audience for an image
e. Explores representations of gender, ethnicity, and other cultural or social identifiers in images
f. Investigates how the audience, context, and interpretation of an image may have changed over time

3. *The visually literate student identifies the physical, technical, and design components of an image.*

Learning Outcomes

 a. Describes pictorial, graphic, and aesthetic elements of an image (e.g., color, composition, line, shape, contrast, repetition, style)

 b. Identifies techniques, technologies, or materials used in the production of an image

 c. Determines whether an image is an original or a reproduction

 d. Examines an image for signs of editing, alteration, or manipulation (e.g., cropping, color correction, image enhancements)

4. *The visually literate student validates interpretation and analysis of images through discourse with others.*

Learning Outcomes

 a. Participates in classroom and other discussions about images

 b. Seeks expert and scholarly opinion about images, including information and analysis found in reference sources and scholarly publications

 c. Informs analysis with discipline-specific perspectives and approaches

Standard Four

The visually literate student evaluates images and their sources.

PERFORMANCE INDICATORS

1. *The visually literate student evaluates the effectiveness and reliability of images as visual communications.*

Learning Outcomes

 a. Evaluates how effectively an image achieves a specific purpose

 b. Assesses the appropriateness and impact of the visual message for the intended audience

 c. Critiques persuasive or manipulative strategies that may have been used in image production to influence interpretation

 d. Evaluates the use of visual signs, symbols, and conventions to convey meaning

 e. Analyzes the effect of image editing or manipulation on the meaning and reliability of the image

 f. Determines the accuracy and reliability of graphical representations of data (e.g., charts, graphs, data models)

 g. Evaluates images using disciplinary criteria

2. *The visually literate student evaluates the aesthetic and technical characteristics of images.*

Learning Outcomes

 a. Evaluates the aesthetic and design characteristics of images (e.g., use of color, composition, line, shape, contrast, repetition, style)

 b. Evaluates the technical characteristics of images (e.g., resolution, size, clarity, file format)

    c. Evaluates the quality of image reproductions, based on indicators such as color accuracy, resolution, manipulation levels, and comparison to other reproductions

3. The visually literate student evaluates textual information accompanying images.

Learning Outcomes

    a. Evaluates information that accompanies images for accuracy, reliability, currency, and completeness

    b. Uses observation of visual content to evaluate textual information

    c. Verifies information that accompanies images by consulting multiple sources and conducting research as necessary

4. The visually literate student makes judgments about the reliability and accuracy of image sources.

Learning Outcomes

    a. Assesses reliability and accuracy of image sources based on evaluations of authority, and point of view or bias

    b. Makes judgments about image sources based on evaluations of image and information quality

    c. Critiques how an image source may create a new context for an image and thereby change its meaning

---

Standard Five

The visually literate student uses images and visual media effectively.

PERFORMANCE INDICATORS

1. The visually literate student uses images effectively for different purposes.

Learning Outcomes

    a. Plans for strategic use of images and visual media within a project

    b. Selects appropriate images and visual media aligned with a project's purpose

    c. Integrates images into projects purposefully, considering meaning, aesthetic criteria, visual impact, and audience

    d. Uses images for a variety of purposes (e.g., as illustrations, evidence, visual models, primary sources, focus of analysis)

    e. Uses images for subject-specific and interdisciplinary research, communication, and learning

2. The visually literate student uses technology effectively to work with images.

Learning Outcomes

    a. Uses appropriate editing, presentation, communication, storage, and media tools and applications to prepare and work with images

    b. Determines image file format, size, and resolution requirements for a project, and converts images accordingly

    c. Edits images as appropriate for quality, layout, and display (e.g., cropping, color, contrast)

3. ***The visually literate student uses problem solving, creativity, and experimentation to incorporate images into scholarly projects.***

Learning Outcomes

    a. Experiments with different ways of integrating images into academic work

    b. Uses visual thinking skills to clarify and solve problems

4. ***The visually literate student communicates effectively with and about images.***

Learning Outcomes

    a. Writes clearly about images for different purposes (e.g., description, analysis, evaluation)

    b. Presents images effectively, considering meaning, aesthetic criteria, visual impact, rhetorical impact, and audience

    c. Discusses images critically with other individuals, expressing ideas, conveying meaning, and validating arguments

    d. Includes textual information as needed to convey an image's meaning (e.g., using captions, referencing figures in a text, incorporating keys or legends)

    e. Reflects on the effectiveness of own visual communications and use of images

---

Standard Six

The visually literate student designs and creates meaningful images and visual media.

PERFORMANCE INDICATORS

1. ***The visually literate student produces visual materials for a range of projects and scholarly uses.***

Learning Outcomes

    a. Creates images and visual media to represent and communicate concepts, narratives, and arguments (e.g., concept maps, presentations, storyboards, posters)

    b. Constructs accurate and appropriate graphic representations of data and information (e.g., charts, maps, graphs, models)

    c. Produces images and visual media for a defined audience

    d. Aligns visual content with the overall purpose of project

2. *The visually literate student uses design strategies and creativity in image and visual media production.*

Learning Outcomes

a. Plans visual style and design in relation to project goals
b. Uses aesthetic and design choices deliberately to enhance effective communication and convey meaning
c. Uses creativity to incorporate existing image content into new visual products

3. *The visually literate student uses a variety of tools and technologies to produce images and visual media.*

Learning Outcomes

a. Experiments with image-production tools and technologies
b. Identifies the best tools and technologies for creating the visual product
c. Develops proficiency with a range of tools and technologies for creating images and visual media

4. *The visually literate student evaluates personally created visual products.*

Learning Outcomes

a. Evaluates personally created visual products based on project goals
b. Evaluates personally created visual products based on disciplinary criteria and conventions
c. Reflects on the role of personally created visual products as a meaningful contribution to research, learning, or communication
d. Validates personally created visual products through discourse with others
e. Revises personally created visual products based on evaluation

---

Standard Seven

The visually literate student understands many of the ethical, legal, social, and economic issues surrounding the creation and use of images and visual media, and accesses and uses visual materials ethically.

PERFORMANCE INDICATORS

1. *The visually literate student understands many of the ethical, legal, social, and economic issues surrounding images and visual media.*

Learning Outcomes

a. Develops familiarity with concepts and issues of intellectual property, copyright, and fair use as they apply to image content
b. Develops familiarity with typical license restrictions prescribing appropriate image use
c. Recognizes one's own intellectual property rights as an image creator

    d. Identifies issues of privacy, ethics, and safety involved with creating, using, and sharing images

    e. Explores issues surrounding image censorship

2. *The visually literate student follows ethical and legal best practices when accessing, using, and creating images.*

Learning Outcomes

    a. Identifies institutional (e.g., museums, educational institutions) policies on access to image resources, and follows legal and ethical best practices

    b. Tracks copyright and use restrictions when images are reproduced, altered, converted to different formats, or disseminated to new contexts

    c. States rights and attribution information when disseminating personally created images

3. *The visually literate student cites images and visual media in papers, presentations, and projects.*

Learning Outcomes

    a. Gives attribution to image creators in citations and credit statements to acknowledge authorship and author rights

    b. Includes source information in citations and credit statements so visual materials can be reliably found and accessed by other scholars and researchers

    c. Cites visual materials using an appropriate documentation style

ABOUT THE AUTHORS

NICOLE E. BROWN is the Multidisciplinary Instruction Librarian at New York University, where she teaches research workshops to a variety of user groups and works to expand and strengthen the teaching role of librarians. She has given presentations and workshops, has led professional development training on four continents, and has written for *Library Journal* and *Internet Reference Services Quarterly*. Her research interests include innovative teaching practices and incorporating new literacies into teaching and learning environments. She holds an MLIS from Pratt Institute.

KAILA BUSSERT is the Foundational Experiences Librarian at California Polytechnic State University in San Luis Obispo, where she leads a foundational information literacy program. Her research interests center on the role of visual literacy across the disciplines of science, technology, engineering, arts, and mathematics. She holds an MA in Near Eastern Studies and an MLIS from the University of Arizona.

DENISE HATTWIG is Curator of Digital Collections at the University of Washington Bothell Library, where she collaborates with faculty and students on digital scholarship projects, facilitates digital collection and repository development, and teaches archiving and interdisciplinary image use. Her research interests include student participation in digital collections, intersections of digital scholarship and repositories, visual literacy, scholarly communication, and data curation. Denise is lead author of ACRL's Visual Literacy Competency Standards for Higher Education. She holds an MA in Art History from the Institute of Fine Arts at New York University and an MLIS from the University of Washington.

ANN MEDAILLE is the Assessment Librarian at the University of Nevada in Reno where she coordinates library assessment efforts, teaches information literacy and research skills, and serves as the library liaison for education, art, anthropology, theatre, and dance. She holds an MA in Theatre from the University of Colorado at Boulder and an MLS from the University of North Texas. She has published articles relating to library instruction, visual and media literacies, information behavior, and reference services.

INDEX